Tools of the Time Traveler

Christopher Feldt

Published by Christopher Feldt, 2024.

While every precaution has been taken in the preparation of this book, the publisher assumes no responsibility for errors or omissions, or for damages resulting from the use of the information contained herein.

TOOLS OF THE TIME TRAVELER

First edition. July 30, 2024.

ISBN: 979-8227554499

Written by Christopher Feldt.

Also by Christopher Feldt

Tragedy and Triumph: A North Georgia History Compendium
Tools of the Time Traveler

Watch for more at https://www.northgeorgiahistory.com.

Tools of the

Time Traveler

Using trees, plants, rocks, maps, computers, and more to explore forgotten places in North Georgia History.

Table of Contents

Dedication

This book is dedicated to my fellow explorers and supporters who believed in me, even when I did not. In particular, I would like to thank David Bevel Jones, Jack Carey, Angela Reinhardt, Blake Moss, Dan Pool, Bill Cagle, Maria Boling, Tim Day, Carla Tatum Horton, Chuck Robinson, Dan Bell, Brooke Reeve, JoAnne Gracey, Wayne Riley, Gerald Sampson, Claude and Michelle Winter, Robert and Janet Calhoun, Sheila and Colin Thompson, Betsy and Nick Solino, Marzena Curtis and her husband James. Special thanks go to Anthony Young for recognizing the value in my research and encouraging me to publish, and for Nancy Davis's incomparable editing skill.

Cover photo: Christopher Feldt

On the cover: Angela Reinhardt stands before a shade tree, a natural indicator of a homesite.

Foreward

All around us are remains of the past that help us to appreciate who we really are in many ways. These stories are comic, dramatic, gigantic, heroic, historic, mystic, and sometimes even cosmic! Learning about these hidden worlds around us is, for each and all, a great adventure!

In this new volume, Chris Feldt does more than tell us about our beloved Pickens and Cherokee counties but garnishes his well-illustrated discoveries with solid advice on exploring and maps, as well as with poetry that makes these events and people particularly relevant.

Chris provides the historical reality to places where I have passed many times without knowing their significance beyond place names and people who became legends that were whispered in passing. Many of these stories are dark, and some not included here should still wait for a time before being public.

The past does not need to be 5,000 years old to be lost or reduced to fable. Much of this history explored, and sometimes recovered from the forgotten, is hardly a century old. Some tales here I have never heard or read elsewhere.

Sit down in the quiet of the evening, alone with something good to drink, and join this adventure! Then dream—or plan—your own journeys and research.

Remember, however, the greater evolving story here, that with so little time in our world and archives, historic sites, and libraries closing or cutting back, whatever stories will be discovered could well be in what little makes it on the internet.

Robert S. Davis

Blountsville, AL

June 20, 2024

Robert Scott Davis has more than 2,000 publications dealing with genealogy, history, records, and research, most of which deal with the state of Georgia (USA) in some form or fashion. He has been widely quoted by or appeared in CNN, Time, Smithsonian, Newsweek, the Wall Street Journal, and elsewhere.

Introduction

While finishing my first book, I realized other stories needed to be told. I had only used about 40 percent of my existing material at publication. I also received feedback that some people had difficulty in visualizing the locations of the events in my first book. Therefore, in this book, when appropriate and not forbidden for reasons of privacy, **I've included the latitude and longitude of various historic sites at the end of each passage.**

This volume contains interesting, peculiar, and harrowing history: a fabled gold mine, the drowning of Woodrow Wilson's brother-in-law in Cherokee County, an abandoned cemetery and church ruins, the antebellum daughter that inspired Mitchell's *Scarlett O'Hara*, murders and accidental deaths tied to one piece of land, sundown counties (places where only whites were allowed after dark), the history of the KKK efforts and how they influenced vigilante groups, a chicken contest that changed the starting and/or ending location, of the Appalachian Trail, and more.

In the afterword of *Tragedy and Triumph*, I stated,

"The good, bad, and ugly all have their place. History cannot be erased by pretending it didn't happen, or by changing the narrative. Once the past transpires, it is etched in stone, immutable and timeless. To remember the history and travails of our ancestors, we can learn from their hardships ....and with a little courage and compassion, do our best not to repeat the mistakes of our darkest hours.

This book delves deeply into those uncomfortable spaces and some stranger ones. Regardless, some lessons we were never taught in school are still awaiting discovery. With this and my subsequent books, I hope to illuminate more of those forgotten chapters.

I end with four tutorials on how to find and explore old historic sites on your own: one, by using trees, plants, springs, and other natural means to find them; two, by using aerial photography in conjunction with old topographic maps. Another by using LiDAR to remove the canopy of trees and vegetation from view so you may find roads, trails, and manmade structures. And the final piece demonstrates how all methods, when used together, can provide an incredibly robust system for discovery, learning, and teaching.

Until we meet again.

Christopher Feldt

Jasper, Georgia

2024

Stranger than Fiction?

What we've thought to be true

may not be at all.

Beware of the Siren

and her treacherous call

Beckoning us ashore

to an illusion of safety,

into rocks of pretense

with our paper boat navy.

The lies of the future

hide in the past.

But the ocean is deep

and the falsehoods are vast.

Will telling the truth

earn your words glory,

if people are suckers

for a good story?

Part 1
Stranger Than Fiction

The Moving of the Appalachian Trail, the Oglethorpe Monument and Free-Range Chickens (1958)

In 1930, Colonel Sam Tate had just built his Tate Mountain Estates, which included his stunning Connahaynee Lodge, Lake Sequoyah, and a beautiful 18-hole golf course. That October, he gathered with state legislators, Georgia's Governor Hardman, and the mayor of Atlanta to unveil the marble monument built by his workers and dedicated to the founder of the colony of Georgia, General James Oglethorpe. They were also celebrating the changing of the name of Grassy Knob to Mount Oglethorpe.

Unveiling of the Oglethorpe monument, October 1930

The ceremony also served another function: beginning that same day, the southern terminus of the Appalachian Trail (AT) began at the monument. From there, one could begin the 2,050-plus-mile trek to Mount Katahdin in Maine. And people did just that. Thousands of people arrived to start their journey. Some would travel east from Tate and then approach from the south, coming through what would later be Bent Tree Drive to the Dude Ranch (located where Bent Tree community's 6th golf hole is) and then from Hendrix Mountain to Mt. Oglethorpe. Others would travel from Jasper via Highway 136 to what then was known as Firetower Road (present-day Monument Road).

As years passed, the Georgia Appalachian Trail Club (GATC) began "blazing" the trees as markers along the way, and hikers stayed at a shelter beneath the fire tower (where the present-day fire station is on Monument Road) that was built by our local Civilian Conservation Corps in 1934. In 1938, the GATC assembled the first sign marking the southern terminus of the AT, after carrying it up in segments from the newly abandoned Dude Ranch to Mount Oglethorpe.

However, the logging industry, vandals, and the growth of the chicken-breeding industry in north Georgia ended up destroying most of the viability of the Oglethorpe section of the trail.

Enter the Chickens

World War II created an agricultural demand for chickens. President Roosevelt's War Food Administration went so far as to seize control over part of the chicken industry. By the time the war was over, Americans were eating nearly three times as much chicken as before. In 1951, a Chicken of Tomorrow contest was held in 42 states to see who could produce a broiler whose meat was so thick you could cut it like a steak.

Charles Vantress, a farmer from California, won the contest. His chicken-breeding method (crossing California Cornish males with New Hampshire females) is still employed today.

By the early 1950s, the start of the trail was overrun by 40,000 free-range chickens that were being bred on the east side of Oglethorpe Road at the 3,000-acre Vantress Poultry

Experiment Farm (named after the above-named Charles Vantress and his successful hybrid chicken) to test their growth, viability, and disease resistance in actual field conditions.

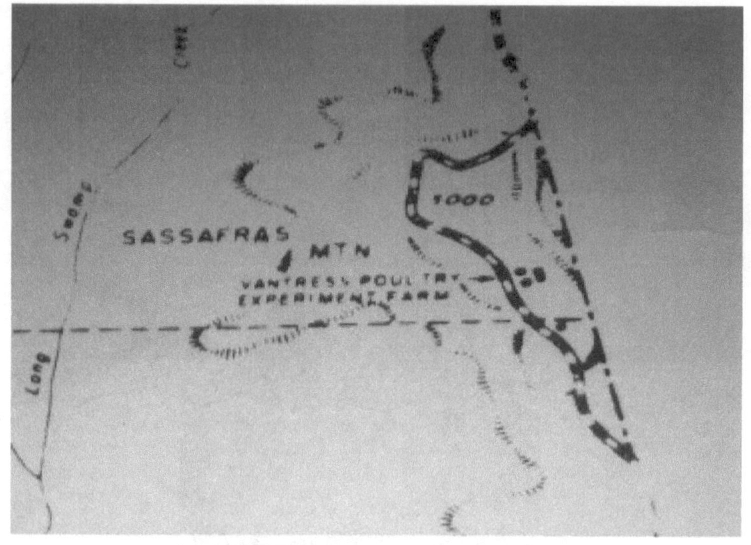

Map showing Vantress Poultry Experiment Farm

The only known photo of the chicken farm in the mountains of north Georgia

The chickens had left so much detritus on the ground that many hikers simply could not make it to the monument without falling into the mess. Additionally, its remote location had made the monument a partying spot for the locals, who left some 50,000 discarded cans of beer and other drinks littered around the area. People were known to use the monument for target practice. General Oglethorpe's face was damaged badly. Horses had done their business at the base of the monument, and as a final albeit unsurprising blow, it was struck by lightning over and over.

Vandalized spire

In 1958, because of the above-mentioned problems (and because the start of the trail was on private land, the start of the approach trail was moved: instead of being through Pickens County, it starts in Dawson County beginning at Amicalola State Park.

By the 1970's, the poultry farm was long gone, as were its thousands of chickens. But the spire still sat at the top of the mountain next to an AT&T tower and other FCC equipment. It had become a relic of a bygone age.

The monument's former location atop Mount Oglethorpe

Finally, after 60 years of being abused atop Mount Oglethorpe, the marble spire was brought down to Jasper in 1998 and restored by a Finnish marble artist named Eino. The once front-facing General Oglethorpe now looks to the side, and a marble ball that once stood atop the monument (missing since the 1960's) was eventually replaced. Today, the spire stands sentinel near the Woodbridge Inn, as a landmark created from Georgia marble, and of the founder of the Colony of Georgia.

Oglethorpe Monument today - downtown Jasper, Georgia.

Grand View Summer Colony, Lodge and Pleasant Valley Lake (1926-1933)

In 1927 H.E. "Cy" Hawkins and his brother (Ira) Tanner Hawkins bought a bunch of land in the Grandview Section of Pickens County, near present-day Grandview Lake. Cy was a former minor league baseball pitcher in Carrollton, Georgia. The brothers wanted to be land developers. Cy was considered the salesman and brains of the operation, and Tanner was the practical builder type. They divided the

into one-acre and five-acre plots. The idea was to sell lots around a resort area with a lodge and a small lake named Pleasant Valley Lake, which was built in 1927. The lake was 15 acres in size and 25 feet deep at its deepest point and was built by damming up a stream. It was stocked with government-issue fish (black bass) brought in from Warm Springs, Georgia. The Hawkins brothers also built small cabins that would come with the land parcels.

Pleasant Valley Lake in Grand View Estates, Jasper, Ga.   Plenty of Black Bass

When Grandview Lodge was nearly finished, Cy arranged for a great chef to come to work at the lodge and to prepare exotic meals for people. Cy started an advertising campaign and advertised in the Pickens Progress, even offering free stays at the lodge with meals included to entice people to buy the surrounding lots. He had a series of postcard-sized cards available that showed various features of the colony as well as the prices involved. His office was located on West Church Street in Jasper, where present-day Pappa's Pizza stands, the site of the former Mary Ann's and before that Arby's.

The Lodge was astonishing. It opened officially on July 14, 1928. It was three stories high, with twenty rooms, French windows, electricity, running water, and a beautiful view of the Blue Ridge and Sharp Top Mountains.

Around 1933, Cy and Tanner packed up their belongings and left. They didn't pay their workers and owed money to many people in the area. They had sold some lots repeatedly and left it up to the buyers to work out who were the real owners. By 1933, many lots were given over to Henry Forest by way of a sheriff's sale.

Eventually much of the land of the Grand View Summer Colony ended up in the hands of the Pickens County Bank, before the bank closed its doors due to financial crisis in 1934. In 1939, the Superintendent of Banks, R.E. Gormley, sold several lots at public auction to liquidate the remainder of what was owed.

In 1946, Mr. Bill Jones and Tracey Mathewson, the world-famous photographer, partnered to create Grandview Estates. The Hawkins lodge needed lots of maintenance and repair, but they quickly got it back into shape. Bill Jones had Champion Creek dammed up and Grandview Lake was created. Two years later, in 1948, the property with the lodge was sold to the Salvation Army, who built a summer camp on part of the former Grand View Estates. The Salvation Army expanded the lodge to house more guests, built a swimming pool, baseball fields and more. It is used to this day.

Tanner Hawkins died of congestive heart failure in 1940. In a fittingly ignominious end, Horace Emmett "Cy" Hawkins was found dead and homeless on a pile of newspapers on the lawn of a Fort Myers Elks Club in February,1953.

Meanwhile, proof that good can arise out of bad was happening back at Grandview Lake. Reverend Roy Blackwell was conducting mass baptism of believers from Sharptop Baptist Church when a photographer from the Saturday Evening Post snapped this locally-famous picture.

In 1958, this baptism at Grandview Lake was conducted by Reverend Roy Blackwell of Sharptop Baptist Church (featured in the Saturday Evening Post)

Coordinates of the former Grandview Lodge (34.4998 -84.3880)

Coordinates of H.E. Hawkins former sales office (34.4667 -84.4236)

The Franklin/Pascoe Gold Mine

Cherokee County officially came into existence in 1831. Previously, the land was known as the Cherokee Territory. Two years before, with the discovery of gold in Dahlonega and Auraria, the second gold rush in the United States took place. (The first gold rush, contrary to popular local belief, took place in North Carolina in 1799.) Shortly thereafter, the Land Lottery of 1832 took place, and residents of Georgia were awarded parcels of land in the old Cherokee Territory. The luckiest were those who won gold lots

Mary Franklin won land near the Etowah River not far from the area of Hightower on the Old Federal Road. With some perseverance and hard work, Mary's gold mine, later known as the Franklin Gold Mine, would grow to be one of the most productive and successful gold-mining operations in Georgia.

The Franklin Gold Mine, Ophir, Cherokee County, Georgia circa 1900

A small community of settlers of European descent, many of them of English heritage, moved into the area and worked the adjacent farms and mines. One of them, John Pascoe, immigrated from England to Canada and then to Cherokee County. He leased ten acres of land around 1835 and opened his own stamp mill. A stamp mill is an ore crushing machine that speeds up the extraction of the desired material. Within a short time, given the success of the Pascoe mine, John had enough money to buy his land and more.

Around the same time, a small Methodist chapel had sprung up south of the mining community. The chapel was named after the Methodist Bishop and circuit rider James Osgood Andrew. Just to the east of the chapel, a large cemetery was built.

Bishop James Osgood Andrew (1794-1871)

Many of the families of the area, especially those affiliated with the Pascoe family and their relations, are buried there. Of the 250-plus graves at the site, only 29 of them are discernable any longer. Early gravestones were made of ~~such~~ low-quality materials that didn't survive the test of time.

Three indecipherable gravestones among of the 250-plus gravestones at the derelict cemetery.

Among the buried are:

John Pascoe (1806-1853)

Mary Pascoe (1859-1863)

Jeremiah Pascoe (1822-1867)

John Moore (1821-1865)

Ann Moore (1814-1876)

Andrew Wilkie (1821-1893)

Mary Wilkie (1826-1856)

Mary F. Wilkie (1864-1865)

Mary A. Wilkie (1821-1898)

Sarah Wilkie (1847-1857)

Abi Wyatt (1857-1883)

Infant Son Hardin (d. unk.)

Bertha E. Hardin (1897-1897)

Bertha R. Hardin (1897-1897)

William Gilstrap (1805-1871)

John Gilstrap (1833-1862)

Merica Dooly (1854-1856)

Thomas Francis (1786-1876)

Malinda Thomlinson (1837-1872)

Mary Donald (1806-1869)

Mary Farmer (1867-1896)

Earnest Farmer (1894-1897)

Harriet McGillivrae (d. 1900)

Edward McGillivrae (d.1900)

Louise McGillivrae (d.1900)

Bety M. (d. unk.)

Tom Floyd (d. unk.)

The small chapel located just west of the cemetery burned down close to the year 1900. Its remains may still be seen in the ground along a flat ridgeline west of an abandoned roadbed. There appear to be old rocks that likely were used as pillars beneath where the floor was, and bricks may be found along the outer edges of its perimeter.

A faint depression can still be seen at the left edge of this photo where the church wall sat.

The descendants of the local families that have remained in the area tell stories of when the Cherokees and white men attended church together at the chapel before the Cherokees' forced removal in 1838. Prior to Mary Franklin's land award, the Cherokee Indians had mined gold at the same location and lived nearby.

Sometime in the 1840s, John Pascoe built a beautiful home (located near present-day Yellow Creek Road in Ophir) near the Franklin Gold Mine. He and his family lived there for some time before John's unfortunate death because of mercury poisoning in 1853. Shortly thereafter, his brother Samuel moved into the home and lived in the area until he passed away in 1887.

Grave of John Pascoe (1806-1853)

Early picture of the Pascoe Home

The Pascoe house in 2023

Later, the Pascoe home became the living quarters of the administrators of the Franklin Gold Mine. The most famous administrator was also the most tragic. In 1905, future President Woodrow Wilson's brother-in-law, Edward Axson, moved into the property with his wife and newborn son. Wilson's first wife was Georgia-born Ellen Louise Axson. On April 26, 1905, Edward, his wife and their son were horseback riding near the old iron bridge when the horses became spirited. Without warning, the horses missed the bridge completely and jumped into the 15-foot-deep Etowah River. Edward tried saving his wife and son, but all of them drowned. Both horses also perished.

Edward Axson

Florence Axson and child Edward Stockton Axson

The three Axson's' remains were transported to Princeton, New Jersey, where they were interred.

Edward Axson's grave, Princeton Cemetery, Princeton, NJ

In 1909, the Franklin Gold Mine was flooded when workers accidentally tunneled too close to the Etowah River. Shortly thereafter, the mining operation was abandoned, and the burials at the old cemetery ceased.

A small school that doubled as a chapel was built around the time the old chapel burned down. However, it too was taken by a fire around 1959. No substantial evidence of its foundation has been found.

A search of deeds and land records at the county list the owner of the land as being the Southern Methodist Conference. Sadly, since the chapel's demise, no one seems to be tending to the property.

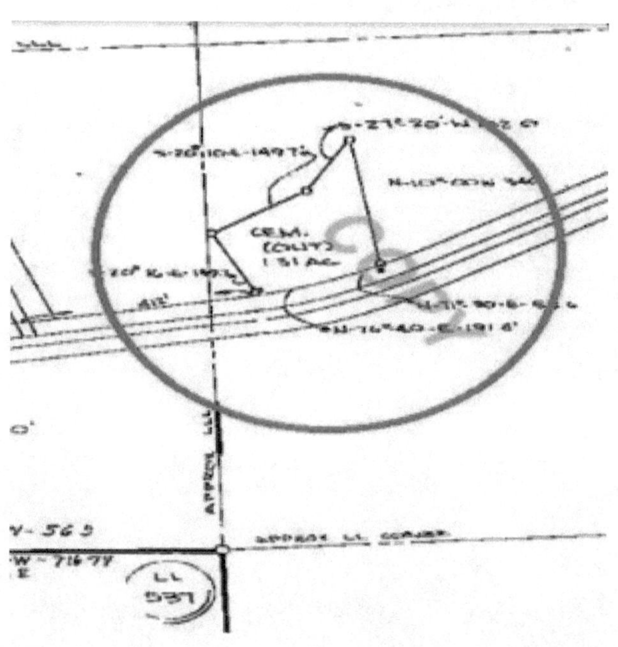

A small plat map of the cemetery

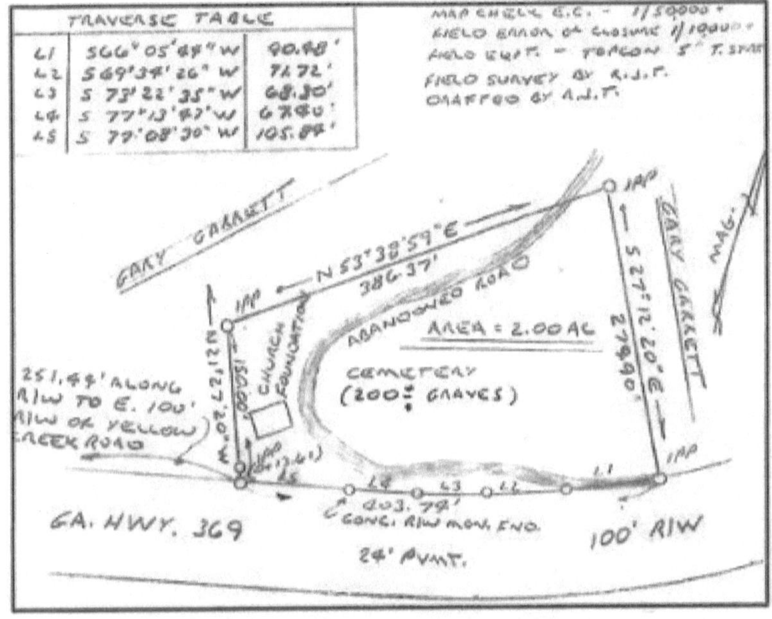

GDOT study site survey map (2007)

Coordinates of Andrews Cemetery

(34.2901 -84.2711)

Coordinates of Pascoe Home

(34.3046 -84.2722)

The Lost Gold Mine of

Pickens County?

In June of 1964, Dr. Joseph Mahan Jr., an archaeologist from Columbus, Georgia, had heard rumors of an abandoned Indian gold mine and wanted to explore it. He arranged a trip to southwest Pickens County, near Henderson and Sharp Mountains, where the mine was allegedly   located.

A man (unidentified) stands inside the mine at the Henson property

To provide some background, in 1878, David Cantrell moved near the Indian Pine section of southwest Pickens County. He lived on the land until he passed away in 1947. His son T.D. lived with him at the property on Route 3, Jasper.

In about 1952, T.D. Cantrell noticed a depression on the side of a hill that looked mysterious to him. He detonated a stick of dynamite and uncovered the entrance to a mine.

The mine was sealed with a rock wall that had concealed it. Upon inspection, the mine turned out to be 5 feet high and 125 feet deep. There were pick marks down the length of the walls, and the mine was flooded with about a foot and a half of water.

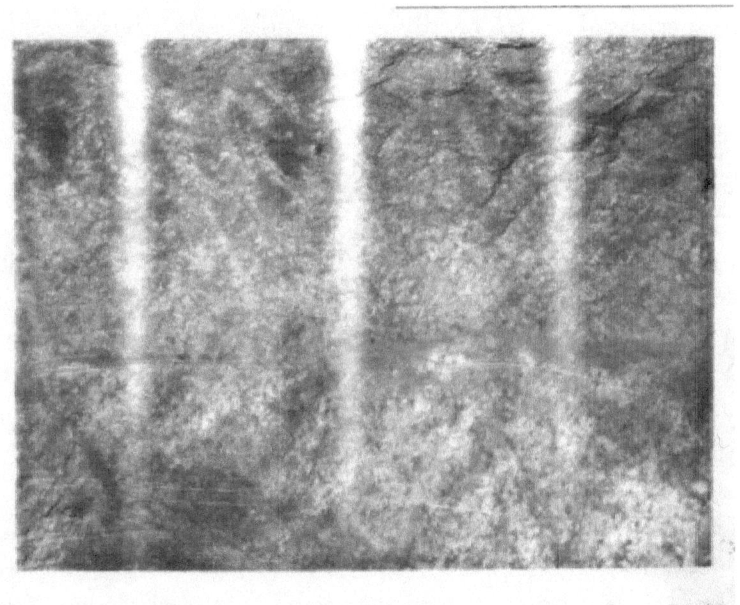

Pick marks in the mine

Reed Henson acquired part of the Cantrell farm from T.D. Cantrell in 1962, and it was he whom the archaeologist Dr. Mahan contacted in 1964. Mahan met with Reed Henson's wife to examine the mine.

Upon investigating, they found two boards made of American chestnut. The chestnut blight of 1904 had eradicated over four-billion Chestnut trees by the 1930s. A neighbor, James Turner, a father-in-law of the Hensons, claimed that none of the original settlers knew of the mine.

In October 1964, Mahan returned for another investigation. He set up a pump and removed most of the water. He also found another possible mine located 50 feet upstream where the landowner had previously discovered three triangular-shaped flint points.

Photos of this second mine were taken, and a quartz vein was found. Mahan speculated it to be an Indian gold mine based on the arrowheads and age of the mine. No gold was found.

Four years later, Joseph Mahan wrote Sam Tate, of Smyrna, Georgia, with details of the mine. He indicated that although he had tried to get the Department of Geology of the University of Georgia to investigate the mine, they never did. Perhaps the lack of evidence provided little incentive to look further.

Mahan was convinced the mine was initially dug by Native Americans. However, he had zero empirical evidence to support his claim: no gold, no Indian artifacts in the mine, no record of Indians having lived on the property.

Mahan unfortunately allowed his own biases to influence his research. For example, he claimed the ancient tribes of Israel visited North America. After reviewing the Bat Creek Stone, an artifact found in Loudon County, Tennessee, he claimed the writing on the stone to be Proto-Hebraic. To Mahan, this proved the Jews discovered America. The stone has subsequently been proven to be a forgery.

(There are many charlatans in the field of history. Some "historians" use dowsing rods, usually a forked twig, to find graves and discern their gender of their alleged occupants and their former ranking in society. Modern science has debunked this method of divination as pseudo-science since its findings are no better than random chance.

In 1902 James Mooney wrote of "moon-eyed people—a group of people who couldn't see well during the day, who built the mysterious rock walls at Fort Mountain in Murray County, Georgia. Mooney attributed this to Cherokee folklore, although other people have traced the origin story to the eighteenth century.

Other "historians" use similarities between the scripts of ancient civilizations to make spurious claims about pre-Columbian Transatlantic Contact Theories.)

Sadly, the truth doesn't always matter when it comes to history. One "historian" told me because I believe in academics, he doubted I would agree with his methods. *I took this as a compliment.*

People are fundamentally suckers for a good story. But to publish dishonest research to sell books is unethical, immoral, and deceitful.

The truth isn't stranger than fiction, it is more edifying.

The Forbidden Fruit

History's replete

with examples of lies.

Most aren't overt,

but cleverly disguised.

The dark side we hide

through sins of omission,

leaves nowhere to run

from the human condition.

What's taken for granted

should not be at all,

when we learn of our mythos

and witness Man's fall.

Part 2
Murder He Wrote

The Discovery of Georgia Marble

(from the stagecoach to the grave)

Henry Fitzsimmons (1790? - 1844)

Folklore tells us that Henry Fitzsimmons, a former stonemason from Ireland, was traveling in a stagecoach along the Federal Road, in what is now Tate, when he was kicked off for being unruly.

While walking from the area near Daniel's Tavern, he noticed an outcropping of marble

Within a short time, Henry began mining marble from the Perseverance Quarry just east of Jasper and crafting monuments and tombstones.

Henry's hand-inscribed monuments can still be found in Lawrenceville, Georgia, and his marble is also found along the railroad tracks in parts of Georgia and Tennessee as distance markers. In his prime, his teams of oxen would carry monuments to far-reaching parts of Georgia and even to South Carolina.

One of Henry's daughters married into the Stegall family and another to a Disharoon, the surname from which Disharoon Mountain takes its name. But, as with many settlers, Henry lived a shortened life. One day in 1844, a mere decade after discovering marble in north Georgia, Henry was murdered. His killer was never brought to justice, and the Perseverance Quarry's ownership passed from his daughter to Colonel James Harrison, who leased the land at the Perseverance Quarry from the Tate family.

PERSEVERANCE MARBLE WORKS, NEAR JASPER, PICKENS COUNTY, GEORGIA.

A few years ago, I visited the wild and unkempt grounds of the Fitzsimmons family plot in Marble Hill. Located on a hill just west of Marble Hill Baptist Church, the gravesites overlook the valley where much Georgia marble has been mined. Henry, his wife, and many of his kin are buried there. The farther uphill you move, the more anonymous the tombstones get. Ostensibly, the bodies of slaves are among unidentified graves.

Unhappy with the condition of the grounds, I arranged for a group of volunteers from Bent Tree's Lake and Wildlife Committee to help clean up the plot. (Bent Tree is the fifty-plus year old community where I live in Jasper, Georgia.) Within a few hours, with a lot of sweat equity and battery-powered yard tools, we restored the cemetery to its former glory.

A clipping from the Pickens County Progress, dated Mar 24, 2022, is shown below.

Bent Tree groups clean historic Marble Hill cemetery

By Chris Feldt
Pickens Historical Society
and Bent Tree
Communications Director

On Saturday, March 19th, nine members of Bent Tree Community's Lake and Wildlife Committee and myself volunteered to clean up the Fitzsimmons family cemetery in Marble Hill. Two years ago, not long before the COVID outbreak, I had approached Lake and Wildlife with hopes of enlisting them to help clean the cemetery. Then COVID happened and everything was postponed.

This last weekend it finally came to pass. Everyone brought equipment, tools, a positive attitude, and a measure of sweat equity to knock this out. Pickens County has owned the land, easy to spot on Marble Hill Church Road, since 2005. Sadly, the cemetery grounds had fallen into disrepair.

Henry Fitzsimmons, an Irish settler of Georgia, discovered a marble outcrop-

Bent tree Lake and Wildlife members (l-r) Andy Kidd, Mary Ada Kidd, Art Tippit, Ken Sinclair, Meghan Wandrie, Steve Hall, Laurie Heern, Robert Chambers, Dora Sinclair at the historic cemetery off Marble Hill Church Road. Chris Feldt not pictured.

See Cemetery on 9A

The giant marble marker commemorating the life of Henry Fitzsimmons.

Henry's tombstone rests in the shade of the surrounding forest.

Coordinates of Fitzsimmons Cemetery

(34.43098 - 84.33650)

A Murder in Bent Tree

The first houses of the Bent Tree Community, a private, gated community located four miles east of Jasper, Georgia, were built in 1970. Today, there are over 1,100 homes. When I moved into the community in late 2018, I was told there had never been a murder within Bent Tree's gates throughout its entire history.

Forever a skeptic, I set out to determine the truthfulness of that statement. In 2022, as we approached the 50th anniversary of the Bent Tree golf course, I invited to the celebration two members of one of the first families who had lived within Bent Tree. When we met in person, I took them on a guided tour of the neighborhood.

Many changes had happened within Bent Tree in the decades since they left, and as we drove around, they were taken back in time as they encountered a place or object that jogged their memories. While driving through the Little Pine and Mole Mountain section, the younger of the two former residents recalled a tragic murder.

In early 1982, Carl and his wife Margery were living in an isolated area of Mole Mountain section, having moved there just two years earlier from Marietta. At the time, Bent Tree was far more rustic and underpopulated, having a mere 150 houses spread across 3,500 acres.

On January 27, Carl called the police. He told the sheriff's department that his 53-year-old wife had shot herself in the head with a .30-06 rifle.

At the crime scene, the Pickens County Sheriff's Department enlisted the help of the Georgia Bureau of Investigation. The GBI was suspicious of the suicide explanation and, upon further examination, determined that Carl had murdered his wife. He was charged with felony murder, and his trial was scheduled for later that year in Pickens County. That October, a jury found him guilty of murder the judge sentenced him to a multi-year prison term, but he was released from prison within a few short years.

After being released, Carl moved away from Bent Tree and gained employment at an Econo-Flash convenience store in Gwinnett County. In October 1986, two men tried robbing him, but they were unsuccessful. He fought off his attackers, suffering cuts to his shoulder and head. When asked about the event he replied, "You betcha I know how to take care of myself."

He proved that more than once. As a former member of the military, he had been trained in weapons and hand-to-hand combat. Violence seemed to follow him wherever he went.

Carl passed away of natural causes on January 18, 1988, and to my surprise, was buried beside his wife, a mere six years after her death.

Death Comes to

Corpsewood Manor

Corpsewood Manor, 1981

The tragic tale of Dr. Charles Scudder and Joseph Odom began in Chicago in the 1960s. Dr. Scudder was a pharmacologist at Loyola University. Charles and Joseph met shortly after Charles arrived in Chicago, when Charles was living with his wife in a mansion on Chicago's West Side. Joseph became his housekeeper. Not long after their kids were grown, Charles and his wife divorced, and he and Joseph became romantically involved. Charles became increasingly disillusioned by the urban and intellectual decay he saw at the university and in his neighborhood, so he decided to live his dream life with his partner. He resigned from the university on his 50th birthday in 1976 and purchased 40 acres on Taylor's Ridge, in Chattooga County, Georgia.

In 1981, Dr. Scudder wrote the following in the April/May edition of Mother Earth News about why he decided to live in isolation,

"After some soul-searching conversations with Joe, I decided that we really needed to find someplace (sic) in hilly country, with the glamour of four seasons but without super-cold winters, with a good supply of pure water and wood for heating and cooking, and–most important–with a measure of isolation. (After years of enduring the sensory overload of city life, I desperately wanted to be situated where I could neither see nor hear my neighbors.)"

And true to his ambitions, he accomplished just that. Within two years, he and Joe had erected their 45,000-brick manor in the woods. They also built a brick gazebo, a three-story chicken coop, a chemical outhouse, a brick house for the 160-foot-deep well, a lake, an orchard, and a garden. They had decided to live off the grid before it became fashionable.

Charles had non-mainstream views about religion, sexuality, and life in general. A lot of this was expressed in his architecture and design plans as well as in his lifestyle choices.

Above the brick gazebo, he placed a giant pink gargoyle. (The gargoyle had once spit water at his former property.) There was a connecting drawbridge that spanned the gulf between the house and the gazebo. Charles and Joe would frequently have tea there while taking pictures of their surroundings.

Charles owned books on the occult, a black and gold statue of Mephistopheles (the demon from German folklore popularized by Faust), a couple of human skulls, and stained glass works of Baphomet and Medusa. Each of the four chimneys of the manor was decorated with a pentacle (a downward-pointing pentagram in a circle). Charles was a member of the Church of Satan, but the CoS aren't devil worshipers. Atheists? Yes. Satanists? No.

His personal art reflected a dark side too. Flanking each side of the entrance to the second floor were two paintings. One was of a baby coming out of the womb and the other of a skeleton baby. Perhaps his most disturbing piece of art was a portrait of himself bound, bleeding, and with a series of bullet wounds to the head. (see portrait below)

Dr. Charles L. Scudder and his bull mastiff

Self-portrait of a gagged and shot Scudder based on a vision that Joseph Odom had.

Police arrive in December of 1982 (chicken coop and Pink Room at the right)

On the third floor of the chicken coop was the Pink Room. The first and second floors were for chickens and storage. The Pink Room was decorated with a mattress, pink walls, whips, chains, and more. It was also known as the pleasure room where Charles would "entertain guests" and share homemade wines from their grapevines and smoke pot, before engaging in sexual escapades.

NOTE: The chicken coop building was built late in the life of Corpsewood. Charles mentioned his plans for building it in his March/April '81 article in Mother Earth News - *A Castle in the Woods.* "...and I designed a new chicken house that I plan to start building soon."

This means that whatever escapades happened there, happened in the last year and a half of Scudder's life.

Dr. Scudder had other affiliations that were viewed suspiciously by locals. They weren't a monogamous couple. Once a month he and Joe would travel to town for supplies. Soon they would begin inviting men to come over for "parties." Scudder would frequently write letters to men in prison and elsewhere about his sexual desires. He even kept detailed notes about what kink each "partner" was into.

Unfortunately, one day they invited the wrong person. Kenneth Avery Brock, known as Avery, was 17 when he met Joe and Charles. He had been hunting in the forest near Corpsewood when they met. He had heard stories about the gay devil worshippers living in the mountains but wasn't afraid of them. Intrigued, upon invitation he visited the manor and the Pink Room. The strong homemade muscadine wine removed Avery's inhibitions when Charles decided to perform sexual acts on him. At the time, the age of consent in Georgia was 14.

However, sodomy was still illegal, even among married couples. Regardless, Avery visited the Pink Room for entertainment on more than one occasion.

Kenneth Avery Lowrance Brock

In late 1982, Avery was living in a trailer with a roommate named Samuel Tony West. West was a 30-year-old felon whose career in crime had started when he executed his two-year-old nephew by shooting him in the head. Over the next several decades, he committed other serious crimes, and by the time he met Avery, he was unemployed and needed a roommate to help him afford to survive.

Shortly after meeting each other, Avery Brock told West of the gay devil worshippers living on Taylor's Ridge, and they decided to visit Corpsewood together. During their visit, Scudder had sex with Avery while West was present. Afterward, Scudder propositioned West, but West got offended and left the property.

From that moment on, the machinations of how to rob Dr. Scudder and his partner began. The gay couple must be rich. After all, they had a mansion in the middle of nowhere, lots of land, a golden harp, tons of antique furniture, etc. The more they thought about it, the better the idea seemed. The gay men were isolated, and no one would hear them scream. However, the men at Corpsewood owned two large English Mastiffs, so the potential robbers would need to bring a weapon.

Samuel Tony West

Avery went on a scouting mission to Corpsewood, but he was surprised when he was denied entry to the manor. Without going inside, he would have had no way to know where any valuables were kept. He also wasn't aware that the manor had no electricity. Avery knew the Pink Room was lit by candles, but he hadn't thought to look for power poles or lines entering the property. He thought for sure the men had money, and he was right, there just wasn't a lot at the mansion. The

Corpsewood couple lived off $200 a month. The rest of their money was kept at the bank. They weren't ones to carry cash.

On December 12, 1982, Avery Brock and West, along with West's nephew Joey Wells and friend Teresa Hudgins, piled into a car and headed for Corpsewood. On the way, they all began huffing Toot-a-Loo (a mixture of alcohol, paint thinner and glue) to get high. After arriving, the four visitors and Charles climbed the ladder up to the Pink Room. Brock and West shared a flask of wine while Hudgins and Wells shared a different flask.

Joey Wells (L), nephew of Samuel Tony West, and Teresa Hudgins (R)

Brock descended the ladder and retrieved a .22 rifle he had borrowed from his mom. When he climbed to the Pink Room again, and confronted Scudder, Scudder wasn't afraid of the rifle. "Bang, bang," Scudder joked.

After about twenty minutes, Brock grew impatient and grabbed Scudder by the hair. Again, Scudder wasn't scared and acknowledged that he'd play along with Brock's game. But next, West tied up Scudder and demanded to know where the money was. Scudder told the truth: all his money was in the bank. At this point, Wells and Hudgins went down the ladder, trying to escape. West went after them and threatened them both. Wells was able to coax West into the car so the three could leave. However, the car wouldn't start, and West forced the group back up the ladder.

Meanwhile, frustrated with not getting anywhere with Scudder, Brock went down the ladder to the manor and demanded that Joe Odom come out with the dogs. Joey Wells, calling down from the chicken house, implored his uncle not to go through with the plan. But his pleas fell on deaf ears. At that moment, a barrage of bullets was heard below. Odom had opened the manor door, and Brock had gunned him down, along with both dogs.

Brock went back upstairs, and the two roommates forced Scudder and the others out of the chicken house and into the manor. Upon seeing his dead lover, Scudder, who was gagged by this point, issued a muffled cry through his restraint. West removed Scudder's gag, again demanded to know where the money was, and asked for a soldering iron with which to torture him. Scudder replied that since they didn't have electricity, there was no point in having a soldering iron.

Scudder tried to check on Odom, with the robbers demanding that he stop. Cryptically he muttered, "I asked for this." (perhaps this was in reference to his premonition of his death) When he refused to stop, West shot him in the face. Scudder persisted in trying to reach his lover before four more rifle rounds hit him in the head. Scudder and the world he had built had come to an end. Joseph and the dogs were no more. Corpsewood Manor, for the first time, contained corpses.

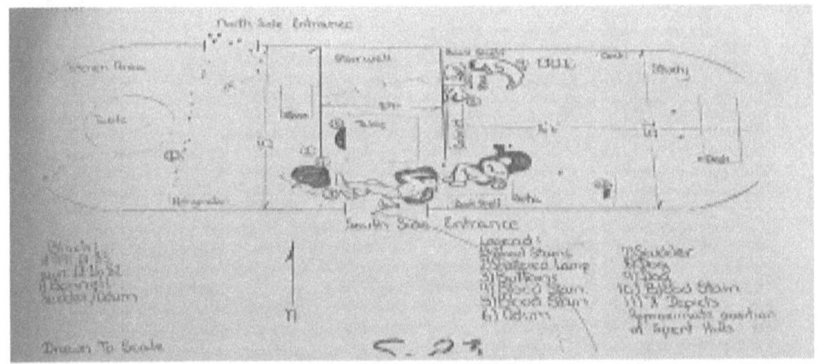

Crime scene sketch by GBI Agent David Bradley Bonnell

Wells and Brock quickly ransacked the manor, looking for any valuables they could take with them. Apart from a little jewelry and a few coins, they found a gold-plated dagger, some silver candelabras, a pistol, and a leather jacket. Since their car wouldn't start, they decided to steal Scudder's jeep. The men also tried to steal Scudder's golden harp, but it wouldn't fit in the jeep. Looking through some final places, Brock was astonished to hear gurgling noises from Scudder, so he shot Scudder between the eyes with the pistol. Joe Odom began moving, so Brock shot him again, completing the callous executions.

The criminals finally got their own vehicle started and fled the property. They weren't happy with Hudgins' desire to tell the authorities, so Wells and Brock kept a close eye on her. They didn't want their uncle go to jail. After four days of being held against her will, Teresa was able to contact her uncle and tell him what happened.

By December 13, Brock and West were traveling through Mississippi and running out of gas and money. They stopped at a rest area to use the restroom and look for another vehicle to switch out. As luck would have it, they noticed a man sleeping in a Toyota next to them. They woke him up at gunpoint and walked him into the woods, where West shot him repeatedly in the head, stole his money, and drove away in his vehicle. Easy money.

Lt. Kirby Phelps, killed for his car by West at a rest stop on December 13, 1982

Three days after the murder at Corpsewood, Sheriff Gary McConnell received a report of strange goings on at Corpsewood Manor. Bullet holes were found in the kitchen door. The dead bodies of the men and the two dogs had left behind an awful smell. The lack of lighting and creepy decor added to the feeling of dread. Around that time, Brock and West began fighting about their escape plans. At first, they had thought they would go to Europe. Then, as reality set in, they set their sights on Mexico. The men were extremely stressed and no longer getting along. By December 18, 1982, Brock ditched West in Texas and began hitchhiking back to Georgia. He eventually made it to Marietta, Georgia, before calling his mom for a ride. The police apprehended him within hours of his making the call.

After separating from Brock, West changed his escape destination from Mexico to Oklahoma. Then he changed it again and traveled from Missouri to Tennessee. Finally, on December 24, he made it as far as Chattanooga and walked up to a police officer with his hands up. He said, "Go ahead and take me in." Unfortunately, the police officer wasn't able to find any warrants in the national system. Regardless, West needed a ride across state lines, and the cop wasn't going to let such an easy catch go.

The officer transported West to the police station in Rossville, Georgia. Meanwhile, another officer called Chattooga County and discovered that West was wanted for the murder of Scudder and Odom. Out of concern for the legality of the transport, the officer drove West back to Tennessee. Georgia authorities from Chattooga traveled to West and booked him in the early hours of Christmas morning.

Within a month of the murders, the justice system of Chattooga County was in full gear. Avery Brock pleaded guilty on February 15, 1983, and was sentenced to life in prison (instead of receiving the death penalty).

Samuel Tony West also pleaded guilty and went to trial in late February 1983. The trial wasn't a long one. Judge Joseph Loggins had a reputation for being tough on criminals. After about a week and a half of trial, the jury decided West's fate within two hours. He was sentenced to death by electrocution.

However, there was a problem with the composition of the jury. The defendant's attorney argued on appeal that there wasn't proper representation by the jury. The earlier court ruling was overturned.

West was to be retried, but instead of going through another costly trial and risking another death sentence, West accepted a plea deal and began serving consecutive life sentences on March 19, 1985.

In late 1983 the manor was burned down by arsonists

After Scudder's estate was settled, West's attorney, Bobby Lee Cook came into possession of Scudder's golden harp, his statue of Mephistopheles, and his self-portrait.

Bobby Lee Cook passed away a few years ago, and the pieces fell into the hands of a private collector in North Georgia.

Bobby Lee Cook with Scudder's Golden Harp. He passed away at 94 in 2021.

Scudder's statue, self-portrait, and harp, today in a

private collection in North Georgia.

As for the Corpsewood Manor property, I recently (February 2023) traveled there with friends and family to inspect the ruins, landscape, and atmosphere.

Coordinates of Corpsewood Manor

(34.554984 -84.241403)

If I had to describe an ambient impression left at Corpsewood, it is one of sadness. I sensed no evil or darkness. It is a sobering place, a place for reflection, for pause. The victims in this crime weren't evil devil worshippers. They were hedonistic and eccentric at worst. Regardless, even if they had been dark occultists, hellbent on worshipping Satan, they didn't deserve what happened to them.

They had families, friends, and lovers. Dr. Scudder had children, and he and Odom were someone's children too. They had interests, desires, and dreams like the rest of us. Tragically, all those things were cut short by real evil. Avery Brock and Samuel West were callous and cold-blooded opportunists with little regard for anything other than how they could get high and profit at the expense of someone else's life. Beyond that, anyone who kills dogs deserves to be in the lowest circle of Hell.

Failure to Maintain

A wooden rail,

with creaky sound,

began to fail

and tumble down

The train fell far

into the valley below.

causing two hearts to stop

of men we know.

The trestle couldn't handle

such tremendous strain.

It would have been avoided

if not for a failure to maintain.

Man's quest for perfection

cannot be completed,

when the strength of his chain

(by virtue of his weakest link)

leaves him defeated.

Part 3
Failure to Maintain

The Trestle Collapse of 1904

The Perseverance Quarry can still be seen on the north side of Cove Road in Pickens County. In the 1850s, two men named Summey and Hurlick operated a marble operation there for a few years.

The operations were stopped during the Civil War. About three decades later, James Harrison of Atlanta, the owner of the Atlanta Printing Company, leased the land near the Perseverance Quarry from the Tate family. Harrison agreed to buy the land for $22,000. However, by 1896, Harrison had only paid the Tate family $1000. The Tate family took Harrison to court and won. It should be noted that the mineral rights to the mine were retained by the Tate family through all of this.

In those days, there was a non-commuter track that ran from Tate, south over Four Mile Creek, to Nelson. The nine-mile section carried newly quarried marble to the finishing plants of Nelson. On November 4, 1904, tragedy struck when James Harrison, the general manager of the Herndon and Atlanta Marble Company, and seven other men were traveling with a marble load from Tate to Ball Ground.

The train was approaching Four Mile Creek and Freeman's Mill over Freeman's Trestle. When it was halfway across the trestle collapsed, and the train and men fell 47 feet to the valley floor below.

The fall instantly killed Harrison and Roadmaster A.C. Gaddis. Engineer Owens was badly injured. Fireman Henry Ingram broke his back. Y.J. Thomason was scalded by steam on his face. And "Bud"

Howard was roughed up. Pat Jordan and his brother Pete were unscathed.

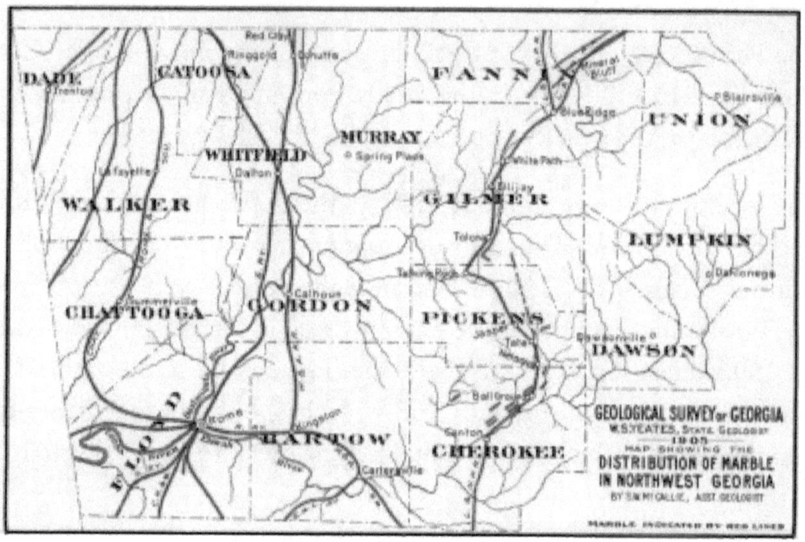

A map from the State Geological Survey of Georgia shows the train line between Tate and Ball Ground, in 1905, still operational one year after the collapse.

The track section above Four Mile Creek

The same track section in 2008

Trestle collapse site with engine in upper third of picture

Coordinates to trestle site

(34.38515 -84.33575)

Coordinates to Freeman's Mill Ruins

(34.35904 -84.33884)

The Tragedies of Steele's

Bridge: Both of them

There were two bridges in north Georgia with the name Steele's Bridge. Now there is one.

Steele's Bridge, 1964 baptism

Most people from Pickens and Dawson Counties are familiar with the metal bridge over the Amicalola River. Spanning 80 feet over a popular fishing and tubing location known as the Devil's Elbow, the bridge has been a landmark of local activity for over 120 years.

At one time, a water-level gauge was installed at the bridge to indicate when flood waters would be approaching. At that time, the nearest post office was listed as Potts Mountain, several miles to the west.

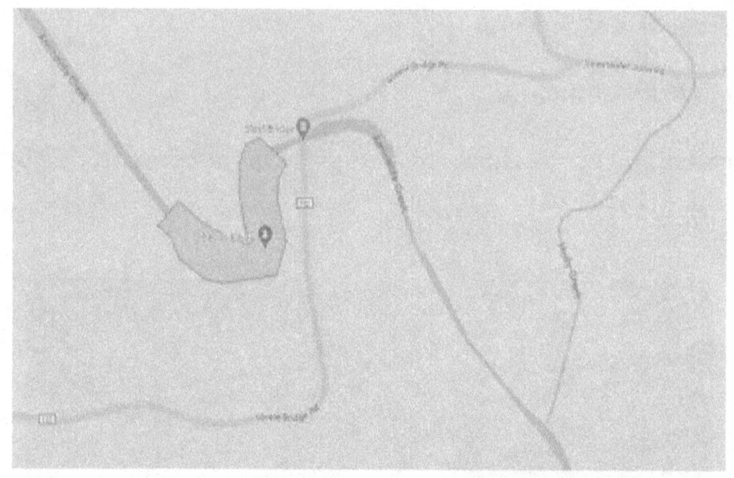

Map of Steele's Bridge, Dawson County

John Henry Chumley, 94, of Dawson County, Georgia, stands beside the ol[d] covered bridge which his father helped build in the 1800s, which crossed th[e] Amicalola River. Mr. Chumley during his youth made whiskey and brand[y] farther up on the Amicalola River, near the Amicoloxia Falls, a Georgia sta[te] park. Mr. Chumley was for many years resident caretaker of the woodlan[d] along the river for the Georgia Marble Company. The covered bridge, inci dentally, burned to the ground in 1978, a victim of apparent arson.

A black and white photo of Steele's Bridge before it was destroyed by arson in 1978

John Chumley and his family helped build the bridge. The Chumleys lived downstream from the elbow, and Wash Steele owned the property upstream. In 1977, the bridge was nominated to be placed on the National Historic Register. At the time, it was one of 22 wooden bridges left in the state of Georgia.

(L) bridge before arson (R) bridge after arson

Arson got in the way of progress. The bridge went up in smoke, a victim of arson. The National Registry application was withdrawn. At one time in the past, the foundations of a bridge that was closer to the river were evident. The new bridge was built another ten feet higher to prevent it from being destroyed by floods.

Today the bridge is metal and covered with graffiti. Like many other artifacts of historical importance, it is marred by the impulsive callousness of morons.

Coordinates of Steele's Bridge, Dawson County (34.455101 - 84.209025)

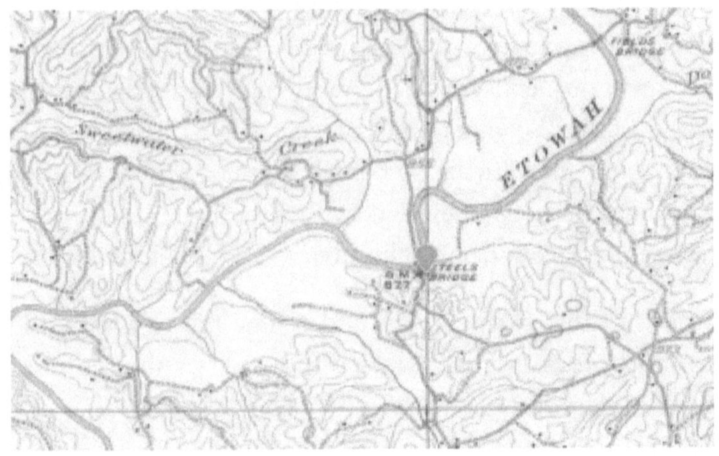

Steele's Bridge, presently under Lake Allatoona

In Cherokee County, another wooden bridge named Steele's Bridge was operational until it was flooded by the creation of Lake Allatoona around 1950. Near Bridge Mill and Steele Bridge streets you can still discern where the roadbed connected to the bridge.

In 1918, at around 1:30 pm, a group of 50 soldiers from Camp Gordon were traveling over Steele's bridge to locate deserters and moonshiners when the first five-ton truck broke through the bridge and flipped upside down. Sergeant Abe Marquis, Corporal Sam Smith, and Private Ernest Rheinsmith died instantly. Private Harold Secord, Private Alfred Tripp, Sergeant Harold Burton, Corporal Edwin Brindley, Charles Kennedy, A.S. Johnson, and George W. Schmidt were all hurt badly. Private Hugh Fitzpatrick, Sergeant Jerald Clune, John Kinen, William Bruck, Lee Bobbett, Corporal Eberhardt, and Neram Price were also bruised.

The driver of the truck, Corporal G.W. Schmidt, despite having a crushed leg and wounded face, helped rescue some of the men.

Another truck was in convoy along with four private vehicles carrying revenue agents, a Deputy United States Marshall, a Selective Service officer, the soldiers' commanding officers, First Lieutenant Mark O. Kimberling and First Lieutenant L.M. Blenner, and the famous war photographer Tracy Mathewson (who several decades later would become one of the founders of Grandview Lake in Pickens County).

They stopped short of the bridge, and several ran to a local house for help. In short order, two doctors and some nurses showed up to help attend to the wounded.

After the truck plunged in, both lieutenants rushed down to the river. They and the uninjured men overturned the five-ton truck to be sure no one was trapped beneath. A nearby resident, Mrs. Carpenter, administered bandages. It took an hour for the ambulance to arrive.

Later Lieutenant Kimberling drove to the home of George Brown, son of former Governor Joseph Brown, to phone headquarters at Camp Gordon. The families of the dead were notified by telegraph. Although the bridge was old, it was found not to have been tampered with.

The bridge collapse in Cherokee County garnered attention for the safety of bridges in north Georgia in many of the newspapers. It was an eye-opener for many.

Coordinates of Steele's Bridge, Cherokee County

(34.1826 -84.5857)

The Ruins

Walking in a forlorn wood,

I stumbled onto something good:

a trapezoid of ages past

that made iron for war by blast.

The men of old that time forgot

left monuments so we would not

go negligently before their works

of giant stones above the earth.

And former stones piled near the draws

where waterwheels once powered saws

and cast downstream to future dreams

of houses built of native beams

Part 4
Antebellum Life

The Iron Foundry Ruins

of North Georgia

Diamond/Fire Eater furnace

This blast furnace was built in 1852 in Bartow County off Stamp Creek. Originally called the Union Furnace, its ownership changed hands more than a half dozen times between its start and 1880. In 1875, this was the first furnace in the United States to produce a commercial, high-quality ferromanganese product at 67 percent purity. (Ferromanganese is used in the steel, foundry, and other industrial production industries.) Its one-time owner, Willard P. Ward, had trained in Europe before venturing into the business in the United States.

In the late 1880s, Georgia was one of only three states that produced any notable amounts of straight manganese ore. The furnace at this site was the most productive of the manganese furnaces in the state.

The site has fallen apart over the last 172 years. At one time there was a wooden race built from the top of an adjacent ridge to safely drop the materials into the furnace from above. The illustration below gives a good representation of the process.

Illustration of an iron furnace in operation

The Diamond Furnace and surrounding land

Coordinates of Diamond Furnace

(34.255325, -84.689371)

Lewis / Oak Grove Furnace (Casting shed side)

The John Lewis furnace, also located within the former Pine Log WMA, was built in 1847, is largely intact in 2024. Another name associated with this furnace is Jacob Stroup. The Stroup family immigrated from Germany to Maryland in the early 1700s. Mathias Stroup learned about iron manufacturing in Germany. He, his son Jacob, and grandson Adam, had built various iron foundries in Pennsylvania and South Carolina. Jacob and Adam Stroup had sided with the colonists in the American Revolution and were masters of iron components for guns as well as bayonets.

Location of former waterwheel and bellows

The waterwheel and bellows would have been installed near the rock formation at the bottom of this photo. The wheel, powered by the creek, would have provided the extra heat necessary to make the iron. Stamp Creek is just out of sight behind where the picture was taken.

Air inlet pipe (Tuyere) for bellows

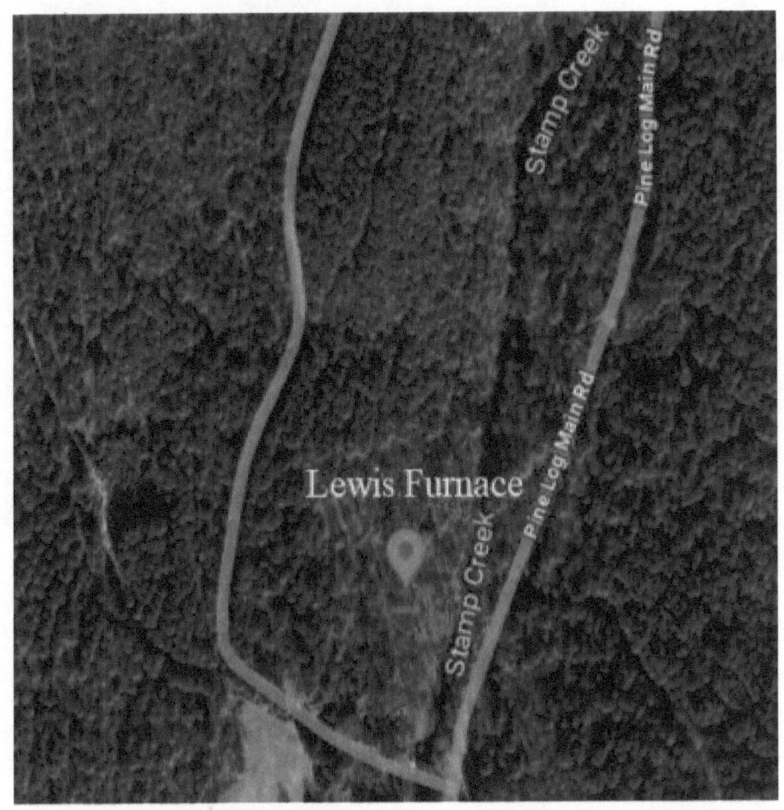

Coordinates of Lewis Furnace

(34.271095 -84.679733)

Jacob Stroup (1771 - 1846)

Jacob's kiln-shaped tombstone

Moses Stroup (1794-1878)

After the Civil War, most of the financial resources needed to maintain and operate iron manufacturing in the area were depleted. By the 1870s, most of the iron furnaces that were built and/or operated were no longer producing anything near their apex capacity of the 1850s. Jacob Stroup died at his home near present Lake Allatoona. His son Moses eventually moved on to Alabama and built his final furnace in McCalla, Alabama.

To reach the Stroup property, one had to hike 1.7 miles each way. When I visited the site in 2020, it was still leased by the state of Georgia as part of the Pine Log WMA. However, today both sites are owned by the Apex Hunting Group, and trespassing is strictly forbidden.

In 2023, a very long lease between the Neel family and the state of Georgia expired. Georgia could not offer as much money as private interests. The last I read, there are plans to develop the 14,000-plus acre parcel into industrial and residential sites. Although there are purported plans for 6,000 acres of greenbelt to be preserved, there is no guarantee the ruins of the iron furnaces will not be torn down in the process.

Two other iron furnace ruins are located with the Pine Log WMA. Poole's furnace and the Bearstack. I never had a chance to visit these sites before the Wildlife Management Area closed.

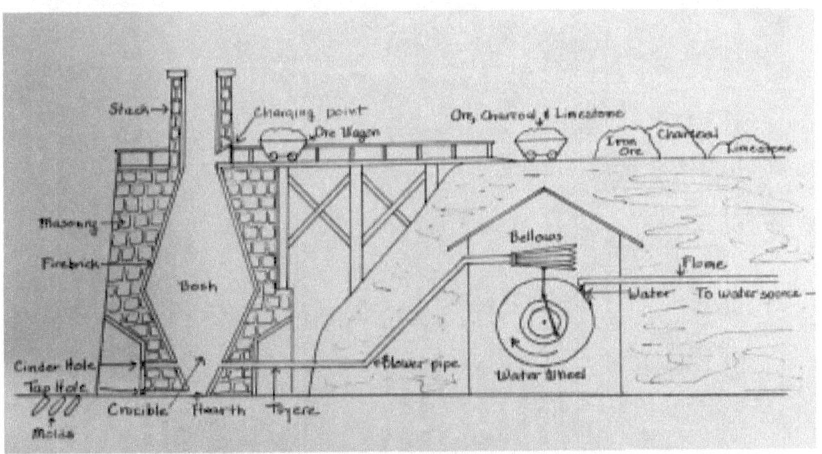

Diagram of a typical pig iron foundry operation

In the diagram above, the molds in the lower left corner are also known as troughs. Hence, the term pig iron. Most items made in these foundries were small and malleable. Utensils, bayonets, and more.

The Paul F. Akin Lime Kiln

A friend stands in front of the arch to give scale to the size of the kiln

Located in Kingston, Georgia, along Limekiln Branch, is the 25-foot-high furnace pictured above. Not much is known about the origins of this kiln. It is shown on Civil War maps. By 1912, it was listed in a Georgia bulletin as the Paul F. Akin lime kiln. A lime kiln is used to make calcium oxide or quicklime powder from limestone. Calcium oxide is used to make cement, paper, and even high-grade steel. Of all the furnaces in this chapter, it is the most easily accessed.

Coordinates of the Paul F. Akin Lime Kiln

(34.246537 -84.913619)

Donaldson's Furnace

Located in Cherokee County on the outskirts of the Georgia National Cemetery are the ruins of the never used Donaldson's furnace. It was built during the Civil War on the southeastern side of Shoal Creek on the land of Judge Donaldson.

My five-year-old daughter Aviana posing on the eastern facing side of Donaldson's furnace.

The interior of the furnace is built incorrectly and is missing a bosh. The bosh is a truncated cone-shaped part of the furnace. It is the hottest part.

Archaeologists postulate the ending of the Civil War may have obviated the need for this site. Also, the water speed of Shaol Creek in the area seems fairly slow. Hence there was no surprise of not finding waterwheel ruins at the site. A final clue about its non-use was the lack of any slag residue anywhere near the site.

The chimney is also missing its necessary firebrick: the insulated coating of the furnace that is refractory and allows for very high-temperature.

Donaldson's Furnace Coordinates

(34.24256 -84.55998)

The C.L. Deal Lime Kilns

In a remote area of wooden forest south of Gainesville, in Hall County, beginning around 1880, a lime kiln was built by the direction of Columbus Lafayette Deal. Built along Walnut Creek, near lots of limestone deposits, the kiln was able to produce around 60 tons of refined ore daily. Eventually the operation expanded, and a second kiln was built, doubling the output capacity.

Kiln A with race connected to the top of the stack.

I recently began looking for this site after Bruce Roberts posted something about it on a website. Bruce loves to share history, but not specific locations. I'm sure he does this out of a desire to protect these sites from vandalism.

After some coaxing, he sent me a small hand drawn map. Between that and the descriptions of the location in old newspapers and Geology journals, I used LiDAR to narrow my search to two areas south of

Gainesville's Airport. **Learn more about LiDAR at the end of the book.**

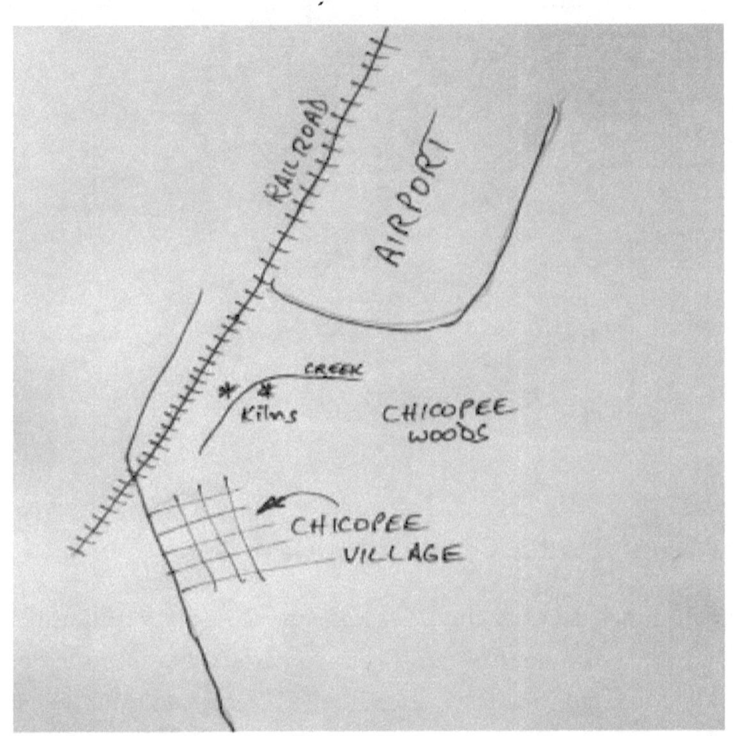

Bruce's hand drawn map

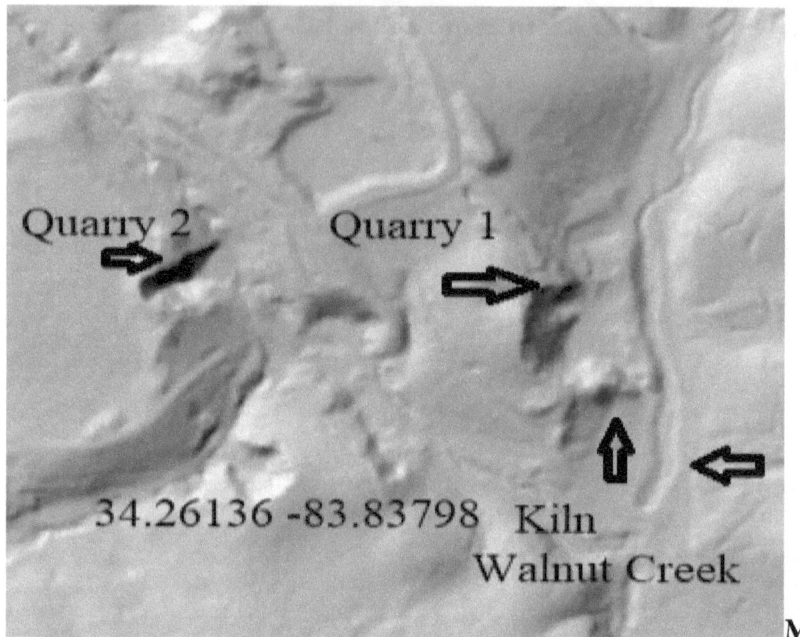

My first guess using LiDAR to find the kiln sites

As it turned out, what I thought was a kiln site was a stack of boulders next to Quarry 1. The quarries are easier to discern because they are larger and leave larger shadows. Manmade objects, unless they are extremely large, are harder to see.

LiDAR guess for Kiln B

Kiln B

A tree grows out of the stack of Kiln B

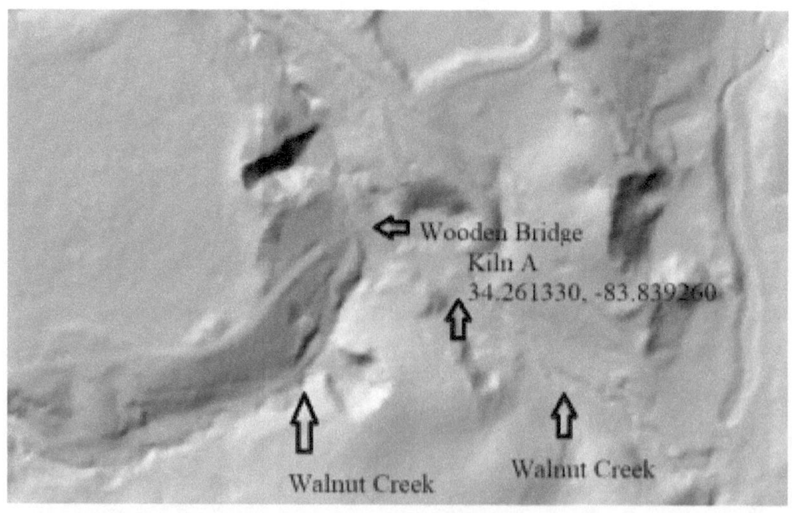

Location of Kiln A, not far from wooden bridge

Aviana stands in front of the NW corner of Kiln A

Only about 30 percent of Kiln A is remaining. The race is gone. The charging shaft is gone. All the outbuildings are gone. The northwest corner is still intact. On the next page my daughter is standing in the far-right corner of the kiln shown on page 100. Just below the knot of the tree on left of the picture, are the remains of metal banding that helped secure the kiln.

A close-up photo of the metal banding remains

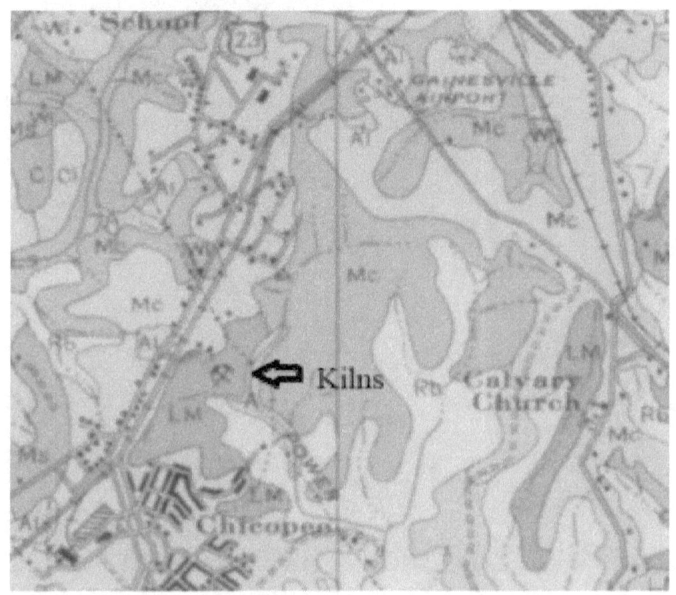

1930s

Conservation map showing mining operation

I recently contacted a descendent of C.L. Deal, after finding them on a Facebook history site for Hall County. They provided me with a picture of Columbus Lafayette Deal and his wife Nancy. I'll be escorting the Deal family descendent to her Great, Great, Great Grandfather's kiln sites this upcoming fall.

The location had faded from their family memory. It is moments like this that make all this research completely worth it.

Columbus Lafayette Deal and his wife Nancy Hughes Deal.

Coordinates of C.L. Deal Lime Kiln A

(34.26133, -83.83926)

Coordinates of C.L. Deal Lime Kiln B

(34.26094 -83.84096)

The Tate Sawmill of

Pendley Creek

In 1850, Tate, Atkinson and Company opened a marble quarry near the present site of the Georgia Marble Company's in Pickens County.

After the Civil War, the Tate family operated a sawmill on Long Swamp Creek in the section that is locally called Pendley Creek. At the time, a main road came north from Tate and bisected the old Dawsonville-Jasper Highway (now Cove Road) before heading directly to the sawmill.

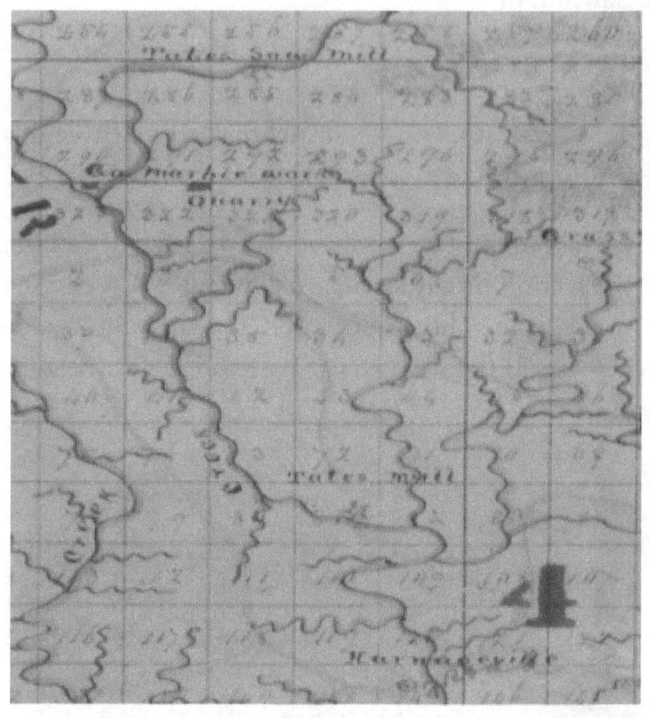

The 1869 Pickens County map by B.W. Froebel is the only one to show this Tate Sawmill.

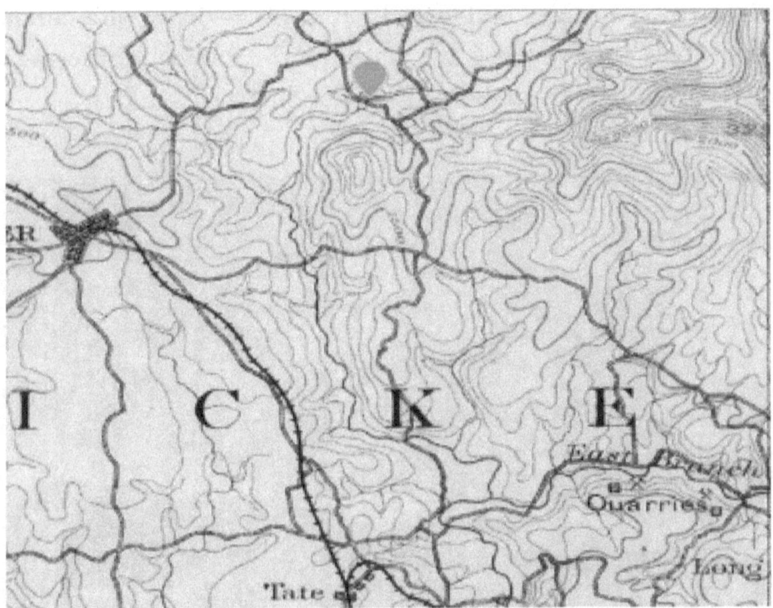

1890 topographic map showing roads and mill location

With a lot of luck and good timing, I was contacted by a neighbor who knew the mill-site property owner who graciously granted me permission to hike in the valley where Long Swamp Creek and the mill site are.

Looking closely at the picture of the ruins, you'll notice several support pillars off to the left. The terraced walls in the center and back center were different levels of the milling operation. Even though the creek is low, the water flows remarkably fast at this site.

In Reverend Charles O. Walker's *Cherokee Footprints* series, he briefly refers to the mill site as the Pendley Mill. If the Pendleys ever owned it, it was after the Tate family, not before.

Further away from the mill ruins is a large foundation of what I presume to be a utility building. There is no evidence of a chimney, and the walls are five feet high. I assume the foundation height was intended to protect the building from flooding.

Large stone foundation, square in shape

Near the site, at the northern fork of Long Swamp Creek, are the remains of a large chimney. Set on a hill to avoid flooding, the fireplace is nearly perfectly intact. It is wider than most fireplaces I've seen in north Georgia. The front of the fireplace is spectacular. Trees have grown up inside what would have been the home's main floor.

An atypically wide chimney

Another site in the area is the Perseverance Quarry (see map below). Presently gated to prevent trespassers, it can be seen on the north side of Cove Road at the so-called S-Curve. (In 1894, James Harrison was the owner of the mine. He died in a tragic railroad accident in Pickens County in 1904. (See the next chapter.)

Note: Perseverance Quarry is within Cove Mountain. Cove Road is named after Cove Mountain and took on the name sometime after the 1940s.

AN OUTCROP OF WHITE MURPHY MARBLE AT THE PERSEVERENCE QUARRY, 2 MILES EAST OF JASPER, PICKENS COUNTY, GEORGIA

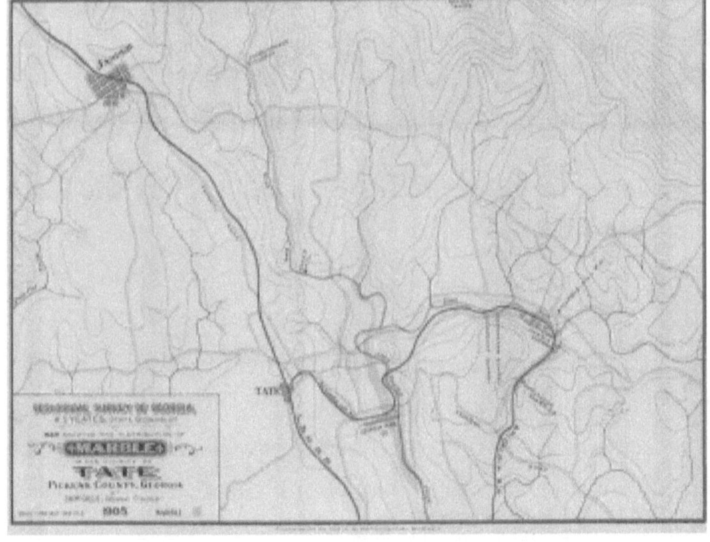

The Keith Plantation of

Cherokee County

The overgrown entrance to the Keith Plantation. Note the main house in the background

According to local sources, the Keith Plantation near Canton, Georgia, in present-day Keithsburg was built during the Civil War. The property was over 3,300 acres along the Etowah River two miles north of the town of Etowah. Etowah was an early name for Canton. The plantation had a large house made of bricks from a kiln using red clay from the Etowah River.

The story goes that the owner of the plantation, Mackey A. Keith Jr., hid food supplies from the Union soldiers when Sherman's men burned down more than half of nearby Etowah. The food was hidden in the trees of the plantation. When the Union soldiers discovered this, they hung Keith from one of those trees in retaliation. In one recounting, the rope broke; in others, the slaves of the plantation cut down their master out of their regard for him. He lived.

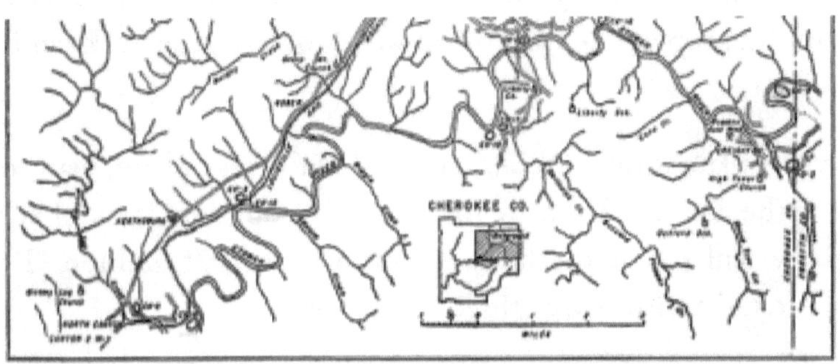

Fig. 177. Cherokee and Forsyth County sites: Hickory Log or Chamblee (Ck-9), Keith Place (Ck-18), Ck-3, Cline Farm (Ck-15), Sharp Mountain Creek (Ck-10), Ck-11, Coker Farm (Ck-19), Smithwick Creek (Ck-17), Long Swamp (Ck-1), Jordan site (Ck-13), Nelson site (Ck-14), Ingram Farm (Ck-12), Conn Creek (Ck-16), Humphrey Farm (Ck-20), Horseshoe Bend (Ck-4), Settingdown Creek (Fo-3).

Archaeologist Robert Wauchope investigated the Keith property in the 1940s. In his report, he claimed to have found evidence of pottery from the Early Woodland Period. There was a village site on the property half a mile past the Keith plantation home along the river. Arrowheads and various stamped and Check-marked pottery types were found at the site. At the time of the excavation, one of the jugs found at the site was of a type that had only been found at one other site in Georgia.

In 1935, the Keith Family sold their land to Pierce Cline. The Cline family passed it on Clyde Teague, whose daughter, Marjorie, married Dutch York after meeting him at the University of Georgia; they moved to the property in 1952. Eventually, the ownership was passed down to the York family.

The York family added modifications to the property, including an in-ground pool and a half dozen outbuildings. Many of the windows and doors were replaced in the home as well. According to sources, there was a fire sometime in the 1980's that ravaged the interior of the home. Marjorie and Dutch York's son Michael currently owns the property.

In 2006, there was a push by the Cherokee County Historical Society to preserve the property as a historical site. However, the York family refused.

Currently, the plantation, outbuildings, and 256 acres of land, many of them along the Etowah River, are for sale. In my opinion, it is unlikely the property will sell at the hefty asking price of $25 million. The owners are in talks with two or three developers.

Today, there are claims of lineage by the descendants of the Keith family slaves. It appears that Mackey A. Keith, Jr., donated 40-acre parcels to many of the intermingled members of the Keith, Bates, and McMickens family lines. Most of those families lived in an area that was known as Keith's Ridge, which later changed to Pearidge.

Phillip Keith donated two acres for the original Hickory Log Church. His wife Aggie was a slave of the Keith Plantation. He is buried at the Hickory Log Cemetery along with his wife.

The Keith Plantation in 1952, facing north

Coordinates of the plantation

(34.252211 -84.450322)

***Keithsburg was originally named Keiths after the surname of the same.**

*One story is that Keithsburg was formerly named Mabel. However, Mabel is shown two miles north of Keiths on the 1894 Marietta and North Georgia Railroad schedule.

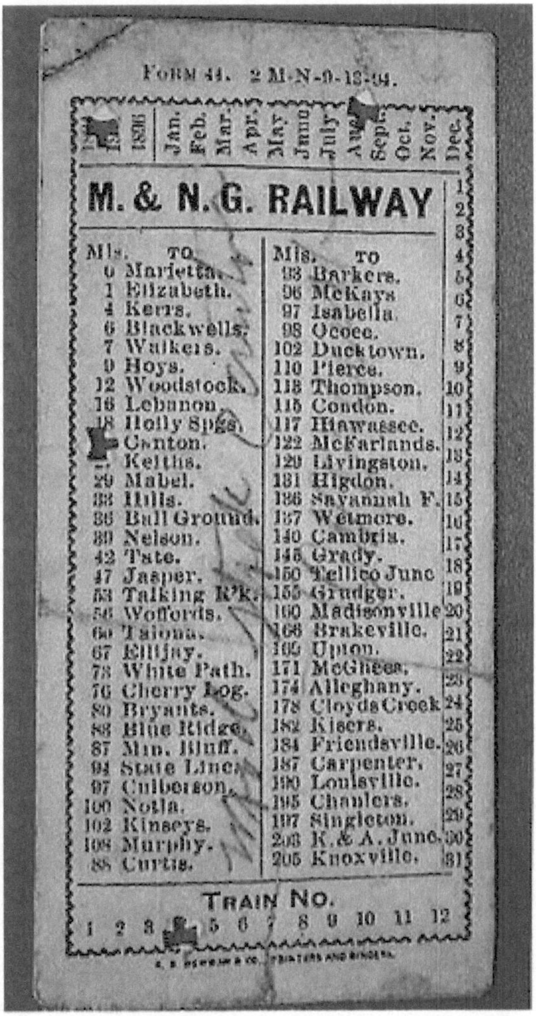

Canton, Keiths, and Mabel as seen on an 1894

Marietta and North Georgia Railroad ticket

Heirs of the Keith family dispersed across the country after they left the plantation. Two of the most adventuresome were the sons of Mackey Keith, John and Amos. John Matthew Keith, born in Lumpkin County, upon turning 18 years old, moved to California around 1850.

He didn't strike it rich in the gold rush. But he got involved in the lumber business in Calaveras County. After that venture didn't pan out, he tried his hand in at farming and raising sheep. As luck would have it, one of his farmlands was rich with oil. He partnered with J.J. Mack and began buying lots of land with oil rights. Shortly before his death, he and Mack sold their land to a wealthy English company named Imperial for $3,500,000, nearly $11,000,000 in today's dollars.

When John Matthew died in April 1914, his estate was besieged by fraudsters. People from all over the country came out of the woodwork pretending to be heirs. The craziest instance of this was when Dr. Susan Tedford from San Francisco challenged the estate, claiming that she was the guardian of a lost heir of John's–an illegitimate child, now a grown woman, from Alaska.

The courts eventually saw through the ruse and dismissed all the fictitious claims. Even John's business partner, J.J. Mack, sued the estate and lost.

Amos Keith

Amos Keith, eight years younger than John, served in the Confederate army. In 1875, he left Canton in search of adventure. At first, he tended to sheep that his brother owned. Later he began working for a Sacramento bank dealing with land investments. Amos was a shrewd trader, buying properties at low prices, and became a well-known landlord in the China Alley section of Selma, California. A kind and eccentric man, Amos had many female suitors, especially after inheriting money from his wealthier brother John.

Shortly before his death, to humor himself, Amos instructed his attorney to read the missives of desperate and conniving women looking for an easy meal ticket. The death and potential fortune of his brother's estate was popular in the news. Women from all over the country would mail him letters explaining why they would be the right woman. One of the letters read:

"Dear Mr. Keith, I have been reading about you in the paper, and have been thinking how lonely you must be, living all alone in the country. I have just finished reproving my sister, who made an unkind remark about you. I told her she should be ashamed of herself to say such things about a good man who has reached the mellow years of life and who should be treated kindly by all the world. I wish that we could meet some time, as I am sure I could bring comfort and solace to your declining years. I shall be anxiously awaiting to hear from you. Yours, very sincerely."

Amos then explained to his attorney,

"You know John, I never believed any of these. I love them all, but I know they are only after my money. I have read Shakespeare all my life, and I have learned a good deal about human nature. Shakespeare was the greatest student of human nature among all the writers and thinkers, and I owe a great deal of my success in life to his teaching. All this has been fun, but I knew there was nothing real in it."

In Amos's will, 48 relatives each got a 2 percent interest in his estate - a small amount compared to what they were expecting.

Amos's will called for his remains to be returned by train to the Keith family cemetery in Canton. Within a week of his death, he was interred in Georgia.

The Keith cemetery in Canton sits on the former land of the plantation across Riverstone Parkway - from the present-day Super Walmart (built on top of the Cherokee Village named Hickory Log). Located directly beside the Waffle House, the cemetery is gated and is still watched over by stewards of the Keith family. The cemetery is beautiful and well maintained. It is on private property and is not open to the public.

The gated entryway to the Keith Cemetery, Canton, Georgia

The Howard Plantation of

Bartow County

Charles Wallace Howard was born in 1811 in Savannah, Georgia. After graduating from college, he attended seminary in Princeton, New Jersey. He was ordained a Presbyterian minister and, in 1838, traveled to England to research the colonization records for the state of Georgia.

Reverend Charles Howard

In the late 1830s, Charles Howard moved to Cass County, Georgia, and bought 800 acres of land north of Kingston along the Conasauga River. During that time the county lines were redrawn, and Cass County became Bartow County.

Howard lived in South Carolina for a time and worked as a pastor at a Huguenot church before moving to Spring Bank, Georgia. In 1852, the Howards opened a school on the property that drew students from wealthy families throughout the area.

The Howard family was wealthy, owned slaves, herded four hundred sheep, had horses, employed private nurses, and more. Within one hundred years, he and his family had, in addition to the school, built a giant home, many outbuildings, and even a natural cement factory with dual lime kilns.

During the Civil War, Charles was a Confederate captain stationed with Hardee's Corps at Dalton, Georgia. In the spring of 1864, the Confederate army retreated and headed to Charles's home. The Confederate soldiers arrived at the Howard plantation, changed clothes, and set up a position a few hundred yards from the house near the railroad tracks. There was a brief skirmish with Yankees in the area, and the Yankees retreated, regrouped, and attacked the Howard plantation. The Confederates fled south four miles to fight at another property. The fighting resulted in 135 Yankees being killed and 18 taken prisoner. When it was over, many of the Confederates made their way back to the Howard estate. By the next day the Union Army retreated.

Later, the Howard home was broken into by rogue Yankees. They stormed the estate, breaking down doors and pillaging each room. Within fifteen minutes they had ruined or stolen many of the items in the house. Some of the men chased the Howard women upstairs. Luckily, an officer arrived and reprimanded his men. Shortly thereafter, another officer arrived to help clear the house. Later, the officers returned to make a list of the damaged and stolen property to compensate the family.

Lithograph of Spring Bank, Charles Howard's 800-acre plantation

The next day, a black housekeeper from an estate four miles away from the Howard estate, told how their property was raided. She had escaped the house and found her way to Union General McPherson. When she described what had happened, that items were stolen and how she was hit by the men—General McPherson made the Union soldiers line up. The housekeeper identified the man who stole her master's watch and demanded it back. Luckily, General McPherson was just, and she got her master's watch back. Instead of being hanged as punishment, the soldier was forced to walk a great distance wearing a ball and chain.

Over the next weeks, Yankees would periodically come and stay at the Howard property. Union soldiers used land for grazing their horses. Nearly all the Howards' helpers had fled. All their chickens and most of their supplies had been eaten or used. For the first time in their lives, the Howard daughters had to take care of themselves. The women were repeatedly bothered by the enlisted men about food. A Union soldier from Kentucky asked them how they viewed the Yankees. The Howard women proclaimed they'd rather deal with a dead Yankee than a live one. In their opinion, dead yanks were harmless.

Nearly six months later, Sherman and his men came to Kingston. On November 7, 1864, while they were there, Sherman received orders from Ulysses S. Grant to march from Atlanta to the sea, leaving destruction in his wake. This was a new type of war for the American military.

Harpers Weekly magazine cover showing Union troops in Kingston GA, 1864

The daughter of Charles Howard, Frances Howard, wrote an account of the Civil War events that took place at her plantation. Titled *In and Out of the Lines*, it wasn't published until 1905.

Several members of the family are believed to have inspired the characters for Margaret Mitchell's *Gone with the Wind*, including Frances's sister, Ella (Nellie) who is thought to have been the inspiration ~~of~~ for Scarlett O'Hara.

Ella Howard, the inspiration for Scarlet O' Hara

The Howard Cement Company, 1911

The cement factory stopped production in 1912 and was closed. Today, ruins of the kilns remain north of Kingston and not far from Spring Bank.

Ruins of the Howard Cement Company

The last daughter and final carrier of the immediate family's surname, Sarah W. Howard, died in 1929. In 1974, the Howard plantation home at Spring Bank burned down. Bartow County purchased 40 acres of the former plantation in 1976 and maintains it as a park for the public.

The family cemetery is located at the site also. There are eleven memorials there.

34.258548 - 84.959220 - Coordinates of Kiln

34.25746 – 84.86176 – Coordinates of Spring House

34.25631 – 84.96195 - Coordinates of Cemetery

The Weakest Among You

The moral duty

of those who lead

is to take care of those

who most desperately need

The food and shelter

they cannot provide,

when born with a handicap

that shatters their pride.

We are not all born equal

with strong limbs that grew.

But for those of us who did,

to the rest of us be true.

You will not be judged

for the selfish things you do.

But rather by how you treat

the weakest near you.

Part 5
The Weakest Among Us

The Poet

Bury me in a nameless grave!

I came from God the world to save.

I brought them wisdom from above:

Worship, and liberty, and love.

They slew me for I did disparage

Therefore Religion, Law, and Marriage.

So be my grave without a name

That earth may swallow up my shame!

> - Aleister Crowley, infamous poet and black magician of
> the mid-twentieth century.

Potter's field - "piece of ground reserved as a burying place for friendless paupers, unknown persons, and criminals" (1520s; early 14c. as potter's place) is Biblical (Matthew xxvii.7), a ground where clay suitable for pottery was dug, later purchased by high priests of Jerusalem as a burying ground for strangers, criminals, and the poor. [Purchased with the coins paid to Judas for betraying Jesus; these being considered blood money it was then known in Aramaic as Akeldema, "field of blood."]

There was a tradition in the United States beginning in the 17th century and lasting through the mid-20th century, for almshouses to be created at a county level to house the poor, indigent, orphaned, elderly, or infirm, and to provide shelter and limited work for those who could not care for themselves, yet weren't criminal enough to be in jails, prisons, or convict camps.

Oftentimes the residents, in conjunction with outside help, operated farms to offset the costs of their stay. The noun "poorhouse" enters the American English language as early as 1781, and "poor-farm" can be found in writings from the year 1834. In Pickens County, the poorhouse was referred to as the Pauper's Home.

The home in Pickens had a farm on the property and was located very close to the county's convict camp. Unlike in Fulton and Cherokee Counties, no record can be found of a poorhouse cemetery in Pickens. Many of the inmates, "upon death, were buried in the city cemetery nearby." If there is a cemetery of unmarked graves, it would be located in District 13, on Land Lot 22 near the line of LL 51.

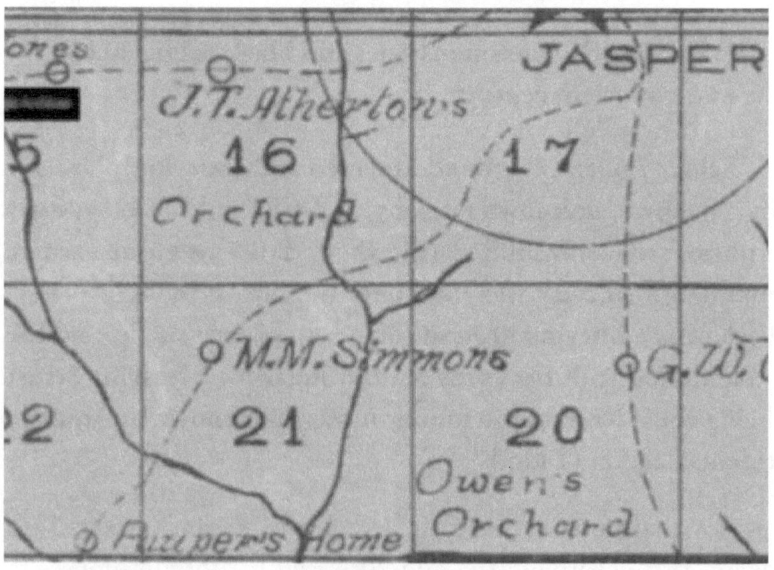

Even though federal census records reflect very few occupants were housed in Pickens' Pauper's Home as each ten-year census was taken, it is likely some folks moved in and out of the homes as vagrants.

Atlanta's first almshouse was destroyed in the Civil War. In 1869, the first records of a Pauper's Cemetery appeared in Fulton County near the present location of Westview Cemetery.

In 1881, the second almshouse in Atlanta was built by convict labor in a rural area near the corner of Piedmont and Peachtree on about 300 acres. In 1889, the pauper's cemetery was moved there.

The March 5, 1905, *Atlanta Constitution* detailed Atlanta Mayor Woodward's order to Police Chief Ball to remove all the misshapen, deformed, and maimed, and get them off the streets and into the poorhouses—the familiar themes of "out of sight, out of mind". Shortly before, laws were passed outlawing panhandling in the city.

In 1911, near present-day Chastain Park, the Galloway House was built as an almshouse for white people. Situated in a 1,000-acre park, it and its sister building, presently known as the Chastain Arts Center, were built nearby to house African American indigents.

In 1911 the Galloway House was built as an almshouse for white people.

The Chastain Arts Center previously was used

as an almshouse for African Americans

In 1934 over 311 paupers were moved to the North Fulton Park site near the present Chastain Park.

During the Great Depression in the mid-1930s, four transient camps were built in Georgia. Three of the four camps were for whites; the only one for African Americans was in Fulton County.

One of the four camps was part of a 400-acre complex in North Fulton Park that would include two buildings to house the homeless.

ONE OF TWO large buildings already erected at the Fulton County Transient Camp, on the Powers Ferry Road, which is being constructed with GERA funds to shelter transients. When completed, the camp will include more than thirty structures, a golf course, swimming pool and other model recreational facilities.

Man Arrested at Macon For Florida Officers

MACON, Ga., Jan. 4.—(/P)—A man booked by police here as Mark Hutchinson was arrested at the local post office at the request of Lakeland, Fla., authorities. Officers from Florida left Macon Thursday afternoon for Lakeland with the prisoner. The Lakeland authorities said the man had escaped from the city stockade.

CHOW TIME AT THE FULTON COUNTY GERA TRANSIENT CAMP. The cooks, who are seen dishing up food for hungry transient laborers, who are building the model camp, are, left to right, Earl Mathews, Welburn Yother and Clark Summie.—Staff photos by Winn.

DEDICATION OF FULTON COUNTY'S NEW 446-ACRE RECREATIONAL PARK, on Power's Ferry Road, which is being constructed by the FERA transient division, Friday afternoon. Left to right, H. V. Brinkman, camp superintendent, receiving the flag which was presented by the American Legion; J. A. Fynn, state transient director; Miss Ada Barker and Miss Mary H. Newell, FERA officials, and F. F. Ahearn, executive secretary of the Atlanta Transient Bureau.—Staff photo by Winn.

NAMELESS GRAVE BOASTS WREATH

At the Fulton County potter's field, the graves were

dug by prisoners from nearby convict camps

144

CHRISTOPHER FELDT

dug by prisoners from nearby convict camps

An article from the *Atlanta Constitution* in 1949 describes a typical occupant of the graveyard.

He was just a tired and dirty old man who failed to rouse and move along when patrolmen on the morning watch flashed their lights over the alleyway where he sprawled.

His worldly goods consisted of 17 cents, a streetcar token, a crumpled pack of half-smoked cigarettes, and the unwashed clothes on his back.

The coroner's verdict was 'acute poisoning - drinking denatured alcohol.'

They never learned his name, although his wizened old body lay in the Grady Hospital morgue for six days while reluctant undertakers and welfare workers attempted to trace relatives, friends...anybody who would shoulder the burden of his burial.

Because no one came forward, he is lying today with others of his derelict legion - the friendless, the suicides, the unwanted - in Atlanta's potter's field. There was no funeral service beforehand. There were neither mourners nor flowers at the graveside.

The mortician's assistant explained: 'The county only pays up to $50....You can't hardly bury a dog well for that!'

By the middle of the 20th century, due to the creation of many programs like the Social Security Act, WPA, and state-run mental institutions, the number of almshouses and people who would live in them declined rapidly.

Much to my surprise, unmarked graves of slaves, the indigent, children, and others who could not fend for themselves have been discovered throughout north Georgia, and, I suspect, the United States.

The following is a non-comprehensive list of a few of the unmarked gravesites discovered in north Georgia since 2014:

- In 2014, The Chastain Park Conservancy Group, the group that aims to preserve the two almshouses and other places of historic importance within Fulton County, hired a company to use ground-penetrating radar (GPR) to search for unmarked graves. The company discovered 86 of them. Most of them were adjacent to the fifth green of the park's golf course.

- In 2016, in nearby Cherokee County, near Sunnyside Cemetery in Canton, 136 unmarked graves were found using GPR near where the county's former poorhouse was located.

- In 2019, at the Sugar Hill Baptist Cemetery, Gwinnett County, 130 unmarked graves were discovered using GPR in the oldest part of the cemetery dating back to 1886.

- In 2022, over 230 unmarked African American graves were discovered by using GPR at Mt. Hope Cemetery, Dahlonega, in Dawson County.

- In 2023, near Island Baptist Church in Sugar Hill, Gwinnett County, over 25 unmarked graves of slaves were found using GPR.

- In 2024, 67 unmarked graves were found in Ellijay, Gilmer County, on a land lot that had housed a church in the 1800s.

*The materials for building the transient camp in Commerce, Georgia, were taken from CCC Camp 1449/P-77 in Pickens County at the end of 1934. In another twist, H.V. Brinkman, the man on the far left of the park dedication photo, was one of the civilian leaders of Camp 1449 and a native of Jasper.

The Sundown Counties

of Georgia

A history of violence used to protect tradition and fight against a centralized economy and power structure can be found in the historical record over a great span of time. A common perception is that nearly all, if not all, the violence committed by groups of vigilantes was inspired by racism. This was largely true, except for the anti-revenuer groups in Georgia during the late 1800s.

After the Civil War, the southern economy was struggling. Many farmers of north Georgia depended heavily on their cash crop, i.e. fruit and other materials used to make whiskey. This was especially true in the small-population counties with mountainous terrain. Unlike other parts of the state, Pickens, Gilmer, and Fannin Counties had no railroad access until the early to mid-1880s. Between the War of 1812 and the Civil War, distilleries had not been routinely taxed. When the taxes were reinstated, many farmers viewed them as a burdensome intrusion into their lives and livelihoods.

The freeing of slaves added another layer of competition for the southern farmer. Freedmen still worked in the fields, but now required pay. And while many did not own their land, they were free to work for whoever would hire them. After 1865, your neighbor might have had a former slave of yours as a hired hand. As history teaches us, the scarcity of resources invariably increases tension.

Eventually, likely taking the lead from the Ku Klux Klan of Murray County, northern vigilante groups took on different names, but with similar organizational structures. Captains, lieutenants, and other officers and regular members were assigned pseudonyms. As with the original KKK, they all took blood oaths.

In Murray County, the group was called the Distillers Union; in Gordon County, the Gordon Grangers; in Gilmer County, the Working Men's Friend and Protective Organization; in Pickens County, the Honest Man's Friend and Protector. In other counties, the names of vigilante groups have been lost to time.

Looking at the census data in other Georgia counties you'll discover that Cherokee, Cobb, Dawson, Fannin, Forsyth, Hall, Towns, and Union Counties had precipitous drops (23% in Cherokee County) in their African American populations between 1900 and 1920.

This is when Sundown Counties came to be. By definition, a Sundown County is one in which a person of color, usually black, needed to be out of the town before sundown. It was implicitly or explicitly known to be dangerous to be there after dark as a minority. There were many Sundown Counties throughout the United States through the 1960s. Some cities are even considered Sundown Cities. Thousands of these cities sprung up across the entire country at the turn of the 20th Century. This merely wasn't a southern phenomenon, but happened largely in areas outside of the south after the Great Migration took place.

An important sidestep is required to understand what happened with the formation of the KKK, its disbandment, and the creation of these groups to fill a vacancy before the rebirth of the KKK in 1915.

The Ku Klux Klan was formed circa 1866 by former Confederate veterans in Pulaski, Tennessee. The Klan was organized into groups in other southern states, calling themselves the Invisible of the South, and, in 1867, Confederate General Nathan Bedford Forrest became its first Grand Wizard. The Klan reached its zenith of power around 1870.

The United States Congress, in response to the atrocities committed by the Klan, passed the Force Act of 1870. Four enforcement acts passed within a few years. They enabled punishments for those who interfered with African American voters, jurors, and officeholders. The acts allowed for the suspension of habeas corpus, thereby allowing the military to arrest suspects without charge.

Nathan Bedford Forrest

These acts, mostly enforced in South Carolina, effectively dismantled the original KKK.

However, in 1915, a former preacher from Alabama was inspired by the silent film *Birth of a Nation*. On Thanksgiving Day, 1915, he led a group of 15 men with a burning cross to Stone Mountain in DeKalb County to celebrate the beginning of the new Klan. He remained in charge of the new Klan for eight years before being unseated by a new leader.

Sadly, *The Birth of a Nation* was the first film ever shown in the White House, and when adjusted for inflation, it remains one of the highest grossing films of all time.

Also coinciding with the KKK period was the use of convict labor as a new form of slavery. (Later in life, Nathan Bedford Forrest had convict workers working his farm.)

After the Civil War, prisoners were on loan to the highest payer for work outside of prison. Many of the north Georgia railroads and other buildings, both government and private, were built by convict labor. Many counties in Georgia and other states had convict camps that were located near the county's poorhouses/farms for widows, children, and the indigent.

Convict wagons in Pickens County

Many of the convicts were Freedmen who were incarcerated for minor crimes. In Georgia, there were felony and misdemeanor camps. Originally, many of the convict camps put their prisoners in chain gangs. In 1907, outrage at the practice of southern states' use of chain gangs morphed into different terminology. While county poorhouses were largely eradicated because of the Social Security programs started in the 30s, the practice of using convict labor continued into the 60s.

All these practices were nothing in comparison to public lynchings that happened throughout the 19th and early decades of the 20th centuries. Lynchings weren't restricted to the southern states, although the South led the field in sheer numbers.

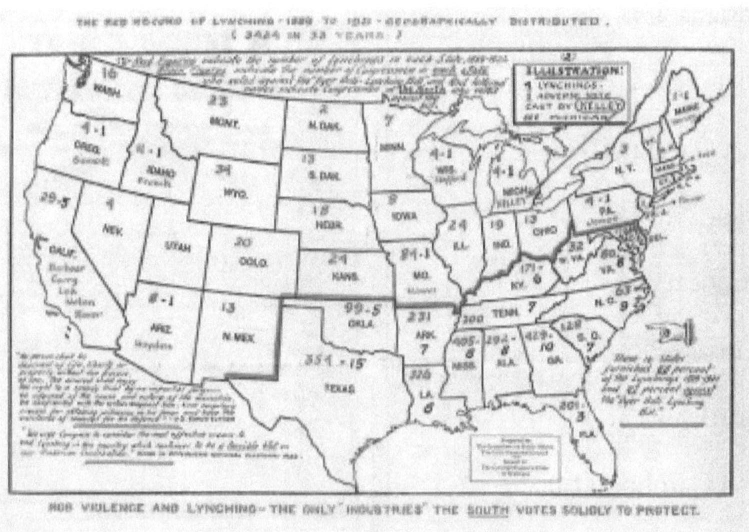

Lynching Map, 1889-1921

A six-year study published in 2017 by theEqual Justice Initiative found that 4,084 Black men, women, and children fell victim to "racial terror lynchings" in twelve Southern states between 1877 and 1950, besides 300 that took place in other states. During this period, Mississippi's 654 lynchings were number one in all that occurred in the Southern states and the United States at large.

Table: Black victims of lynchings per 100,000 Blacks, by state, 1882-1930 (from *A festival of violence: an analysis of Southern lynchings, 1882-1930* by Tolnay & Beck, 1995, pg. 38) State No. of victims per 100,000

Mississippi 52.8

Georgia 41.8

Louisiana 43.7

Alabama 32.4

South Carolina 18.8

Florida 79.8

Tennessee 38.4

Arkansas 42.6

Kentucky 45.7

North Carolina 11.0

Several anti-lynching bills were passed by the northern states in the 1920s; however, they were all blocked from passing by a coalition of southern legislators. It wasn't until the 1930s that an anti-lynching bill was passed, and yet no one was prosecuted successfully until the mid-1940s.

Lynchings persisted even beyond 1950, with 1952 being the first year with no lynchings reported.

Since 1909, over 200 anti-lynching bills were introduced that failed to pass. However, in 2022, an anti-lynching bill, largely in response to the outrage over the murder of George Floyd, passed in the U.S. Senate and House of Representatives.

Perhaps the best example of a sundown county is Forsyth County. In 1912, several blacks were lynched and hung in front of the county courthouse, with some sources claiming at least 5,000 attendees. Shortly after, night riders drove off all of Forsyth County's African Americans. This violence spilled over into Dawson, Cherokee, and other nearby counties.

In Cherokee County, the arson of the Coggins farms on *December 5, 1915, resulted in the loss of 160 livestock and 16,000 bushels of corn, as well as hay and numerous farm implements. Coggins employed a great number of African American workers.

Coggins' Crescent Rock Barn

In another of the seven arsons that happened that week, the livestock of Otto Springer were switched out with "plugs" (less healthy and financially viable cattle), and his farm was destroyed. Four of his real cattle were found grazing on Burnt Mountain in Pickens County a few weeks later.

In Pickens County in the 1910s, Colonel Sam Tate of marble fame, aware of the threat from KKK groups, armed his men and prevented the gangs from forcing out his African American workers at Georgia Marble. Shortly after Colonel Tate died in 1938, many of the African American workers in neighborhoods like Smokey Hollow, Upper and Lower Whippoorwill, and Lonesome City moved away to the North, looking for meaningful work.

Some of Colonel Tate's workers

In the 1860s, the British began investing heavily in cotton farms in Egypt and India. The cotton market became oversaturated, and the former high price of cotton was no longer attainable. Additionally, the economy of the South was devastated by the Civil War, and prosperity among the average farmers was rare.

An outbreak of "Whitecapping" occurred in the Mississippi counties of Amite, Franklin, and Lincoln. Secret vigilante groups formed to disrupt the merchant-farmer system. When the merchants would foreclose on white farmers, they would bring in Black workers to work the farmers' former lands. The Whitecaps, a Klan-like group, would terrorize the Blacks and force them to leave the farms. In 1893, a group of 100 men stormed the jail of Lincoln County to try and free their imprisoned vigilante friends. However, local officials with the support of Governor John Marshall Stone were able to defeat the movement. Similar raids on jails happened in Pickens (1888) and Forsyth Counties (1912) in Georgia.

The crop-lien system emerged in this environment. Under the system, merchants would loan food or supplies to farmers (mainly Black) for their anticipated yield for the next harvest. In most cases, the crops wouldn't meet the debt and the farmers would continue to owe more to the merchant every year. This cycle would turn the farmers into de facto indentured servants of the merchants. It also would allow the merchants to control which crops the debtor farmers would plant.

The net effect of the system favored the wealthy and the plantation owners. The system consolidated their wealth.

To the poor white farmers of Mississippi, much of their former land was controlled by the merchants and their black tenants.

Between 1902 and 1905, farmers formed vigilante groups to "put the Negro in his place" and force them to work for non-merchant-owned farms. Again, in the Mississippi counties of Amite, Franklin, and Lincoln, hundreds of people joined groups such as the Farmers Protective Association, the Farmer's Industrial League, and the Farmer's Progressive League. The vigilantes came from the ranks of these groups.

It took several years and the support of Mississippi Governor Longino, local prosecutors, and undercover detectives from the Pinkerton Agency to end the groups' reign of terror and influence in Mississippi.

It wasn't until the 1940s that the crop-lien system was no longer used. World War II created many jobs, and poor farmers moved to the larger cities to find work.

Franklin County, Mississippi, is also the county known for the murder of two Black students in 1964. Two men were hitchhiking when they were apprehended, beaten, chained to an engine block, and drowned in the river.

When I began to write about sundown towns and counties, I had no idea the research would reveal how backward our nation had been in its treatment and protection of *all* its citizens.

And yet, looking at the numbers, I'm reminded of Georgia's legacy. It took the entire United States 73 years to kill as many African Americans via lynchings as Georgia did in one year to the Cherokee in 1838. Let that sink in for a moment.

*It is interesting to note that the arsons of both groups not only happened within two days of each other, but that December 5 coincides with the anniversary of the creation of Cherokee County in 1832 from the Cherokee Territory.

The Forsyth County

Lynchings of 1912

At the turn of the 20th century, Forsyth County was mostly rural and white. There were small contingents of African Americans living in pockets in areas like Big Creek, Sawnee Mountain, and Oscarville; for the most part, they were poor and lived a hardscrabble existence. In September and October, 1912, several heinous crimes drew the ire of the white community.

After the slaves of the South became Freedmen, they competed for the same resources as the whites. In times of economic hardship, Blacks often found themselves as targets of racial injustice. Groups of vigilantes appeared not just in the southern states, but throughout the nation. Often referred to as Night Riders, white men would don dark outfits and, on horseback, would harry the Blacks of the United States. Atrocious tactics were routinely used by the Night Riders. Their methods included arson, mutilation, torture, rape, hanging, dragging by vehicles, and excessive gunfire, many of them ending in murder.

In September 1912, a white woman from Forsyth County named Ellen Grice claimed she was "awakened by the presence of a negro man in her bed." Eventually, bloodhounds and a posse headed out in search of her alleged assailant. A teenager named Toney Howell and a few other men were detained as possible suspects.

Word quickly reached the people of Cumming that Ellen had been "assaulted." Tensions escalated and a mob gathered in town. A black preacher named Grant Smith made the mistake of speaking out against the bloodthirsty desires of the throng and was nearly beaten to death.

Out of concern that he wouldn't be able to quell the crowd, Mayor Charlie Harris of Cumming called Governor Joseph Mackey Brown for backup. Two elite units of the state militia, the Candler Horse Guards and the Marietta Rifles, were deployed to keep the peace. To the disappointment of most of the residents in the square, the units arrived and safely escorted the accused away to the jail in Marietta.

A few days later, 15-year-old Mae Crow of Oscarville went missing. Mae was supposed to have walked to her aunt's house, but she never arrived. Mae's father went searching for her at night. Groups of men joined in the search with no success. By daybreak, she was still missing.

By the next day, the worst fears of any parent were realized as Mae was found nearly dead in a large pool of blood and with deep wounds. Soon a 16-year-old Black boy named Ernest Knox was questioned by a white man named Marvin Bell. He was threatened that if he didn't confess, he would be hung. Like the criminal confession practices of medieval Europe, torture and/or the threat of torture to garner a confession was the flavor of the day (at least when it came to the treatment of Blacks.)

After Bell got his confession by placing Ernest Knox under duress (he threatened him with a mock lynching), he drove him to the sheriff in Gainesville. It didn't take long for mobs to form near the jail, and the suspect was moved again, this time to 'the Tower' in Atlanta for safety.

The Tower was the most formidable jail environment of north Georgia, if not the entire state. It was a giant stone fortress with a solidary tower that reached high into the sky. Unlike Forsyth County's jail, its doors and walls were not easily breached.

Fulton County Jail "The Tower"

The citizens of Forsyth, having been robbed of their opportunity to hold someone accountable without the constraints of the law, captured a field worker named Rob Edwards at Marcus Waldrip's property in Oscarville. Sheriff Reid and Deputy Lummus stopped the mob from burning Edwards on the spot and raced him back to the Cumming jail.

His reprieve was brief. After securing Edwards in the jail, Sheriff Reid left Lummus alone with the prisoner and walked out of the jail, through the crowd, and out of sight. It didn't take long for a blacksmith to pry open the jail door with a metal bar and sledgehammer. The mob stormed the jail and dragged Rob Edwards into the square.

Within minutes, he was hanged from a telephone pole, dead, and hundreds of people gleefully shot bullets into his lifeless body.

Not satiated, the crowd headed for Marietta to get vengeance on the remaining suspects of Mae Crow's attack. Sheriff Reid returned to the jail and placed a call to the judge in Marietta, warning him of the oncoming assault. The judge arranged for the teens to be taken to Fulton's Tower and, by the time the mob arrived, the prisoners had been transferred to safety.

The next day, Edwards was cut down and examined by the coroner, who concluded that he died from blunt force trauma to the head and from hundreds of gunshot wounds. Many of the Black residents in the county took the hanging body as a warning to leave the county.

Next, the destruction of a white man's storehouse by arson was interpreted as evidence of an uprising by the local Blacks. Rob Edwards' wife Jane, her brother Oscar Daniels, and a neighbor Ernest Knox were arrested as accomplices in the attack of Mae Crow. Mayor Harris quickly moved them to the Fulton Tower to prevent a repeat of the earlier jail bust and hanging.

Mae Crow

Things grew quiet in Cumming during the day, the trials were postponed, and local life seemingly returned to normal. The same was not so at night. Groups of terrorists would travel around the county threatening the Black families to leave and, in some cases, forcing them to. Then news broke of Mae's death. Within two weeks of her attack, she finally succumbed. Mae Crow was only fifteen years old.

Within a month, more than 20 houses occupied by Blacks were burned down, and five Black churches were destroyed. Most of the Blacks were driven away, with only the few who worked for the wealthy whites staying behind.

The trials of Ernest Knox and Oscar Daniels for the murder of Mae Crow, with Oscar's sister Jane Daniels being tried as an accomplice; and of Toney Howell for the rape of Ellen Grice, were set for October 3, 1912, at the Forsyth County Courthouse in Cumming.

Jane and Oscar Daniels, Toney Howell, Ed Collins, Isaiah Pirkle, Ernest Knox under armed guard at the train station in Buford, Georgia.

The old courthouse in Cumming burned down in 1973

The Governor declared a state of martial law for the area. The four accused and two witnesses were then escorted by the National Guard from the Tower in Atlanta to the train station. They traveled by rail to the train station closest to Cumming, Buford, Georgia. From there, 167 armed troops marched the prisoners 13 miles to Cumming.

A twelve-member white jury was selected for the trial. Among them were two men, who, along with Cumming's Sheriff Reid, would become active members of the local Klan in the 1920s.

After getting little rest the night before, the prisoners were marched to the courthouse in Cumming. Jane, having spoken to the authorities in private the night before, suddenly decided to change her testimony. Now, according to Jane, Ernest and Oscar, as well as Jane's husband Rob Edwards (who had already been killed by the mob), demanded she hold the lantern while they had their way with Mae Crow. The jury found the two men guilt and sentenced them to die by hanging within one mile of the courthouse. The execution was set for October 25.

The military constructed a 100-yard fence to keep the public from viewing the spectacle. The night before the hanging, someone had snuck into the gallows and burned down all the walls that had been put up for privacy. However, the hillside to the back left of Dr. Ansel Strickland's house formed a neat little ring, just high enough to give people sitting on the hills an unobstructed view. (Dr. Ansel Strickland, a descendant of one of the most notable slaveholding families in north Georgia, lived less than a mile from the courthouse. His grandfather, Henry Strickland, moved to Gwinnett County in 1828. At the age of 80, Henry owned 1,800 acres of land.)

The day came, and Ernest and Daniels were hung to death. Neither of them had anything to do with the murder of Mae Crow. Within a year or so, all the African Americans in Forsyth County, 100 percent of them, were forced into exile into adjacent counties. Their houses and properties, if not destroyed by arson, were stolen by avaricious white men.

A giant crowd amasses the execution of Knox and Daniel on October 25, 1912

I visited Dr. Ansel Strickland's home in 2024. Looking at the topographic maps, it becomes clear the executions happened on what is an adjacent property today, but in his time the land belonged to him. He donated the use of his land for the execution as well as the wood for the scaffolding, the gallows, and the surrounding fences. Ansel had no qualms about his feelings about Blacks.In his words, "I say this hanging was a legal hanging, because it was the will of at least half of the citizens."

The Strickland home in 2024 / 212 Kelly Mill Road, Cumming GA

The general direction of where the lynchings took place in 1912

Ode to the Map

A forgotten place.

A former town.

A fragmented sign,

A discarded noun,

The path of a river.

The curve of a sphere.

The height of a mountain.

Aligned objects appear.

Where something once stood

a breadcrumb was left.

The trail became good

for those who are deft.

A picture made clear

on a canvas anew,

was positioned so near

it came into view.

Part 6
Rural Exploration

Rural Exploration – Part 1

(How to find manmade structures with old maps)

Being curious, detail-oriented, and courageous are the most important traits of an explorer. While people can learn how to read maps, look at aerial photography, and determine latitude and longitude, they cannot learn to be curious. Like color-blindness, you're either born curious or not. There are many videos online of urban exploration, a process frequently referred to as urbex. Taking a cue from them, I will illustrate the basics of using its rural equivalent, RUREX, to explore rural areas.

Step 1 – Finding the Right Map

Nearly every inch of the United States has been mapped by the United States Geological Survey in the form of topographical maps.

A topographical map shows land features, ridge lines, hills, mountains, valleys, streams, creeks, rivers, cities, railroad tracks, and the best topographical maps which show building locations as squares. In the following example, I use the Tate Nelson Quadrangle Map of 1926 to illustrate its utility.

The best place to find topographical maps online is at the United States Geological Survey website

https://ngmdb.usgs.gov/topoview/

From here, select "get maps," type in your area, and explore.

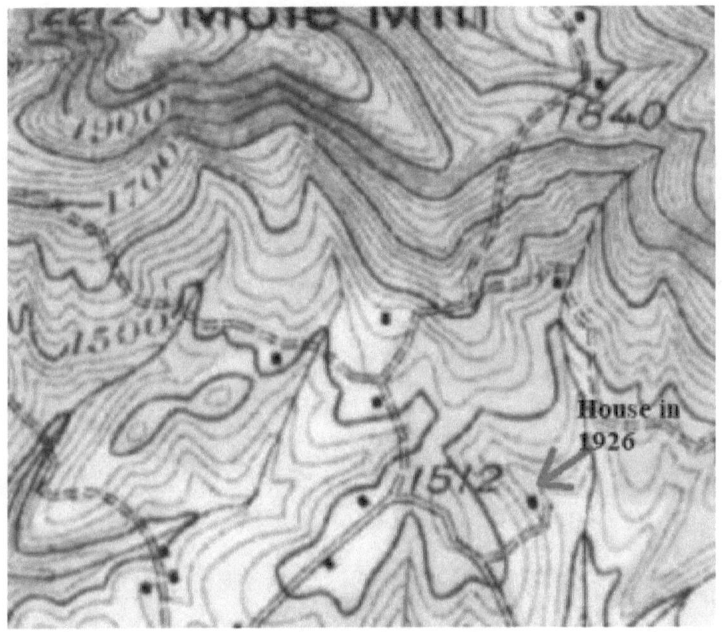

The square dot to the left of the red arrow is the location of a house.

All maps show features that generally don't move much, such as mountains and churches. Believe it or not, streams and creeks, especially in Georgia, change their paths a lot over time. The reason isn't erosion, either. Georgia has so many manmade lakes (reservoirs) and dams that the water pathways of many alluvial bodies have changed dramatically over time.

In the picture above you see Mole Mountain in the upper left. You'll notice there's a road approaching Mole Mountain that splits off to the west and another that goes northeast.

Step 2 – Compare it to Google Maps

Compare your topographical map to Google Maps below. You'll notice some of the same roads are in place and others have disappeared. The road on the map on the previous page beneath the 1512 elevation marker is Long Swamp Church Road. Pendley Circle (in its present form) is not on the topographical map but is on Google Maps.

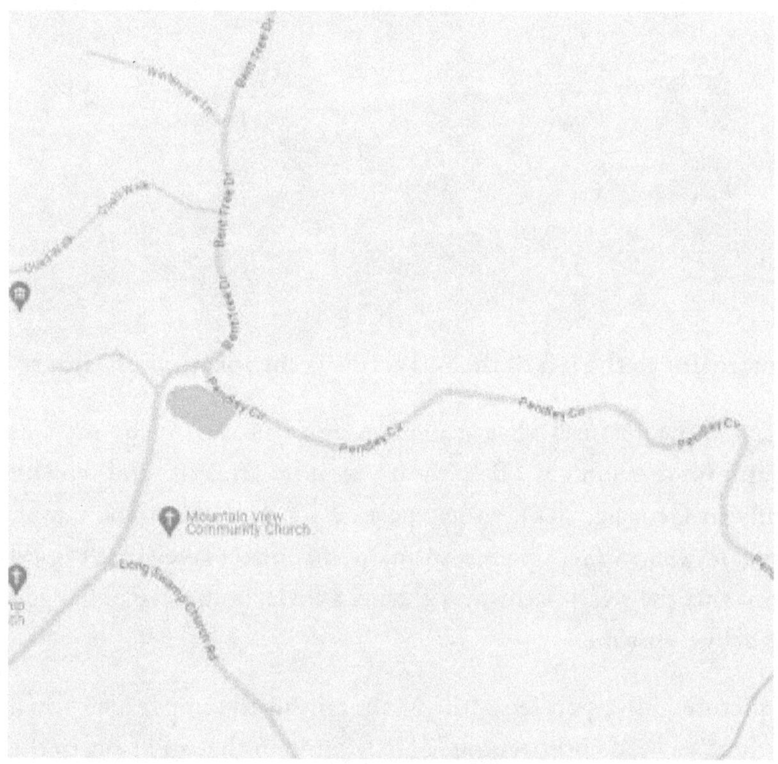

Step 3 – Compare it to USDA Aerial Imagery

In 1938, the United States Department of Agriculture began compositing aerial photos of the counties of north Georgia. These maps are generally available by decade through the 1980s in the

National Archives. More current maps are available through different systems.

1955 United States Department of Agriculture photo of the homestead

Depending on your target location, USDA photographs can generally be found starting in 1938 and updated once a decade through the 1970s. Most of these maps are found at the National Archives located at https://www.archives.gov/. From there go to Research Our Records and then Search the Catalog. For Pickens County, type in "Pickens County aerial photos 1938"

Step 4 – Compare it to Google Earth Imagery

Locally, Google Earth imagery is available going back to 1992 with varying degrees of clarity. Interestingly, the resolution is worse in the 1992 Google image than in the 1955 USDA picture.

1992 satellite photo of the homestead area

Step 5 – Establish Latitude and Longitude Coordinates

Clicking on the exact site with Google Earth will reveal the coordinates of the location. Move your cursor to the area in question and look at the coordinates. In this case, (**34.466765 -84.354597**) (or 34.466765 deg N and -84.354597 deg W) are the latitude and longitude coordinates of the house.

Step 6 – Cross-check the coordinates in Google.

Go to www.google.com and type the latitude and longitude numbers. Click "maps" to reveal the location on a Google map.

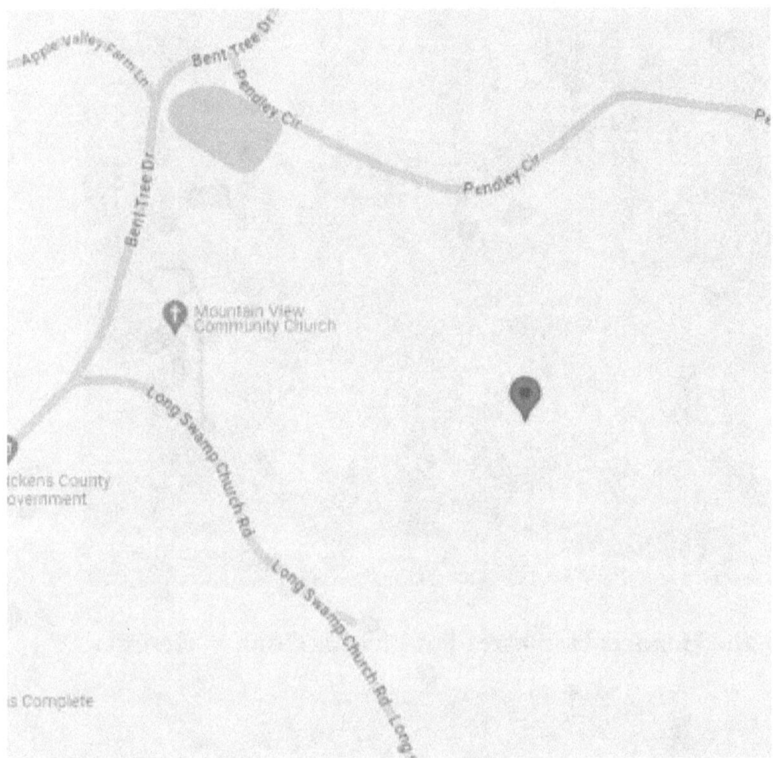

The red dot corresponds to the coordinates found on Google Earth.

Step 7 – Get Permission to Explore

Once you determine a prospective site to explore, use the county land records to determine who the owner is. Contact them and explain your purpose for exploring. Invite them to be present when you arrive. Assure them you will not disturb anything, take anything away, or leave anything behind. No one wants a treasure hunter traipsing around on their land. Documenting places for the historical record is far different!

Step 8 – Explore and Document

The Hendrix Homestead of Pickens County, Georgia

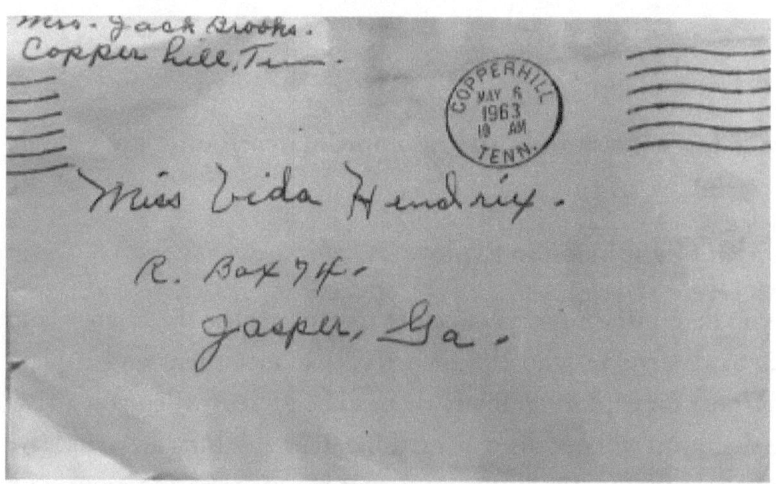

The Brooks and Hendrix families are tightly interwoven. The postmark of May 6, 1963, was just shy of 6 months before the assassination of President John F. Kennedy.

Inside the structure I found correspondence between Vida Hendrix and her kin in Copperhill, Tennessee. **Note:** pay attention to dates found on mail, newspapers, and magazines. The dates may lend clues to the culture and events of the time.

I forwarded it to the original family. Connecting loved ones to their ancestors is one of the most rewarding aspects of this hobby.

I also found a photograph of a young man at the location below. Unfortunately, the water damage to the picture was extensive, and none of his relatives could identify him on a local online forum.

Step 9 – Look at the Legal Description

Looking at legal descriptions can yield interesting clues like the names of former roads or landmarks that may still be present.

This property was formerly known as the Henry Fitts home and was located near the Harrison Pendley property and Long Swamp Baptist

Church. The deed indicates one of the boundary roads was named Settlement Road. Settlement Road likely refers to the original road used by the European settlers of Cherokee County back in the 1830s. Other navigation points are listed as an old pasture fence and creek.

Step 10 – Research the Owners (Note: The deed chain goes back to before 1853, when the property was still part of Cherokee County)

- James Coward (t), Jr. bought most of Land Lot 8 from Sam Tate in 1843 (Cherokee County D.G.B. p 294-295)

- Hiram D. Cowart bought for $200 same from a Robert Cowart (also spelled Coward) in 1872 (Deed book D/202).

- Van Buren Tatum bought for $225 same from Hiram D Cowart in 1874 (Deed Book D/392).

- William Ervin Fitts bought the same in 1893 (i/616) from what looks like his father-in-law Van Buren Tatum.

- Henry Fitts purchased for $3,000 in 1941 (Deed Book W/ page 46) from William E. (D) Fitts

- Ada Hendricks and two of her children purchased the property for $2,050 from Henry Fitts (Deed Book Z/168) in 1946.

Step 11 – Look at Other Maps

The legal description mentions 70 acres of Land Lot 8 touched Harrison Pendley's property.

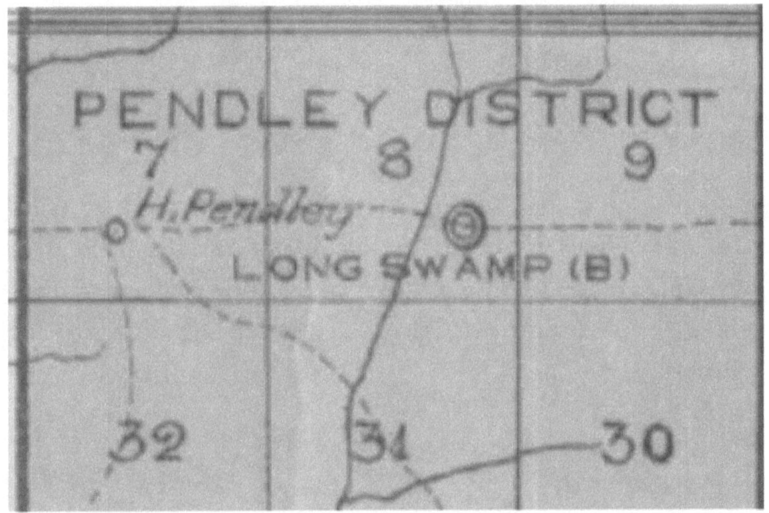

Map showing the roads, Harrison Pendley place and Long Swamp Baptist Church. The Circle indicates a church and the B indicates a Baptist denomination.

Step 12 – Compile

Put everything together and analyze. In this case, I was able to find an old homestead, a spring, a well house and pump, several outbuildings, and an old root cellar. The Cowart, Fitts, and Hendrix families all owned the land and still have relatives in the county. All three families are pioneers in the area. They were aptly found along a settlement road.

The construction on the interior of the home clearly indicated it was built in several stages. A log cabin was built as a small-square-foot area with a fireplace. Later walls were added to the interior to hide the logs. Rooms were added later (presumably as the family grew), each with its own fireplace.

By the 1970s the house was in poor condition, and Bill Hendrix lived outside of the structure in a trailer, next to a propane tank. The only reason the house stands today is because it is supported by fireplaces and trees and has a metal roof.

Final Thoughts

Using old maps to find abandoned structures is an eclectic art. It takes a mixture of attention to detail, land navigation abilities, legal research, technology skills, understanding of topography, knowledge of archival sources, and luck. With a little practice, you also can begin having your own adventures.

Rural Exploration – Part 2

(How to use nature to find manmade structures.)

In the previous section I illustrated different steps and tools you can use to find an old homestead, abandoned cemetery, etc. Now I will demonstrate how to use trees, plants, and other natural features to find formerly used and/or inhabited buildings.

Step 1 – Get Permission to Explore

Follow the same steps as outlined in Part 1: determine who the owner is; contact them and ask permission to explore, explain your purpose, and assure them that you'll not disturb anything.

Step 2 – Explore and Document

Begin by looking for the usual suspects: shade trees

Step 3 – Look for the biggest tree

Drive around on the outskirts of a small rural city. Look for a giant oak, beech, or other hardwood with a high crown and massive trunk circumference. Generally, there is only one, although in rare instances, there are two. Be sure to look for larger trees set back from the road.

Step 4 - Get closer and look for perennials

Once you spot the potential shade tree, move in for a closer look. Spring is a good time to explore, because you may see perennial flowers like jonquils or daffodils in a cluster near the tree. This will be a former garden area. As it turns out, even decades after a house burns down or people move away, the perennials will continue to blossom each spring.

Step 5 - Look for a rock wall or fence

Once you find perennials, you will usually find a wooden fence or small rock wall. The fences generally were used to hold farm animals. The rock wall may contain another garden section or be part of a foundation. Depending on the age of the homesite you're exploring, and sometimes on the wealth and/or industriousness of the former owners, your foundations may be made of stacked field or river stone and held together with mortar. The wealthier the former landowner, the taller, larger, and more elaborate the rock walls will be.

Step 6 – Locate the chimney

Depending on their size and construction materials, chimneys can give away lots of information. For example, two-story fireplaces are rare, but if found in larger-than-traditional homes, are an indication of wealth. The building materials, be they mud and fieldstone, brick, or marble, can tell a lot about the wealth of a homeowner and the geology of the area. They also may indicate different time periods of construction.

Step 7 – Look at the Legal Description

Parcel Number	007B 026
Account/Realkey	22932
Location Address	269 GYM TRL
Legal Description	DIST5 LL114 TRACT D GYM-FRIT2-ORR CAMP
	(Note: Not to be used on legal documents)
Class	A3-Agricultural
	(Note: This is for tax purposes only. Not to be used for zoning.)
Tax District	COUNTY (District 01)
Millage Rate	19.79
Acres	0.84
Homestead Exemption	No (S0)
Landlot/District	114 / 5

Looking at legal descriptions can yield interesting clues like the names of former roads or landmarks that may still be present.

In this case, the name Fritz Orr is the clue. Fritz Orr rented this area of the county for two years in the 1930s and led groups of canoers from the Chestatee to Chattahoochee River before the creation of Lake Lanier. He is famous for his Atlanta-based youth camps and canoeing equipment.

Step 8 - Other

By using the roads and topographic maps, in conjunction with elevation changes, you can take elevation readings on your phone and make common-sense guesses as to how far houses would normally be from the road.

Compare your topographic map to Google Maps. In many cases, you'll notice some of the same roads are in place and others have disappeared.

Step 9 – Compile

Put everything together and analyze. In this case, I was able to find an old homestead, a spring, a well house and pump, several outbuildings, and an old root cellar.

Step 10 - Who lived here before?

By learning who lived on a property and what family they were from, you can learn much about their lives from local genealogy books and websites like ancestry.com and newspapers.com. You may learn about relations, addresses, marriages, military service, schools and colleges attended, social status, etc.

Final Thoughts

As with using maps, using your eyes to find abandoned structures is an eclectic art. It takes a mixture of attention to detail, land navigation abilities, topographic understanding, and luck. However, with practice, you also can begin discovering places and learning more about them.

Rural Exploration – Part 3

<u>Using LiDAR to identify, and verify manmade objects:</u> structures, roads, trails, quarries, etc. beneath vegetation.

What is LiDAR? LiDAR stands for Light Detection and Ranging. It is a remote sensing (usually by airplane) technique that works by shooting pulsed lasers at the surface of objects and measuring the time it takes for objects to reflect back.

This technology allows for high resolution maps to be made of the Earth, moon, and other surfaces. There are many applications for this science. However, we are only interested in it as it applies to archaeology.

To begin, go to the website

<u>https://apps.nationalmap.gov/3depdem/</u>

In the upper left, type your latitude, longitude or address and search.

When the map shows you the area you're looking for, there are about eight different layer types you can use. I prefer using the multi-directional hillshade option.

In the following example, we search for the Georgia National Cemetery in Canton, Georgia. Using the minus button in the upper left side, change the resolution to .4km

We are looking for an indication of where Donaldson's Furnace may be based on information given in two Archaeology reports from the 80s. One by Gregory Jeane (1984) and the other by Garrow and Associates (1987).

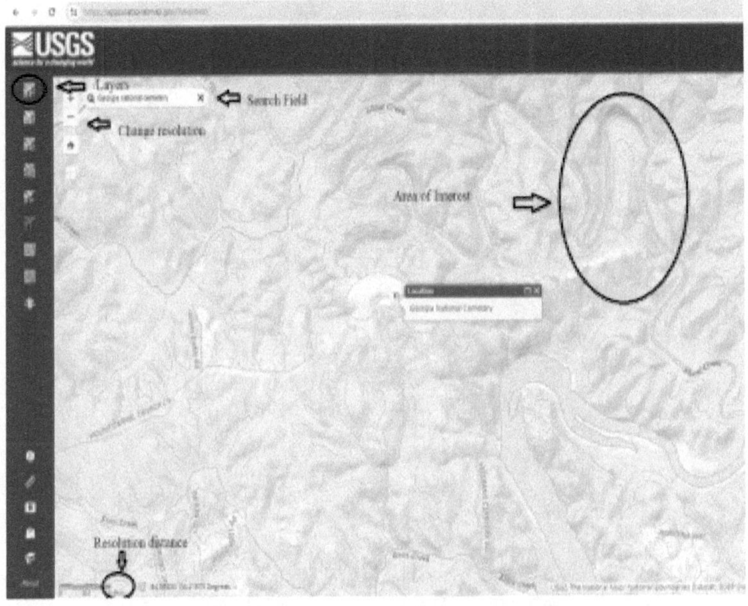

Base map altered to .4 km resolution

In the following example, we search for the Georgia National Cemetery in Canton, Georgia. Using the minus button in the upper left side, change the resolution to .4km

Click on the hillshade layer and move to the area of interest.

Notice how clear the trails and paths to the furnace become. Also notice the only manmade structure in the area is the furnace object.

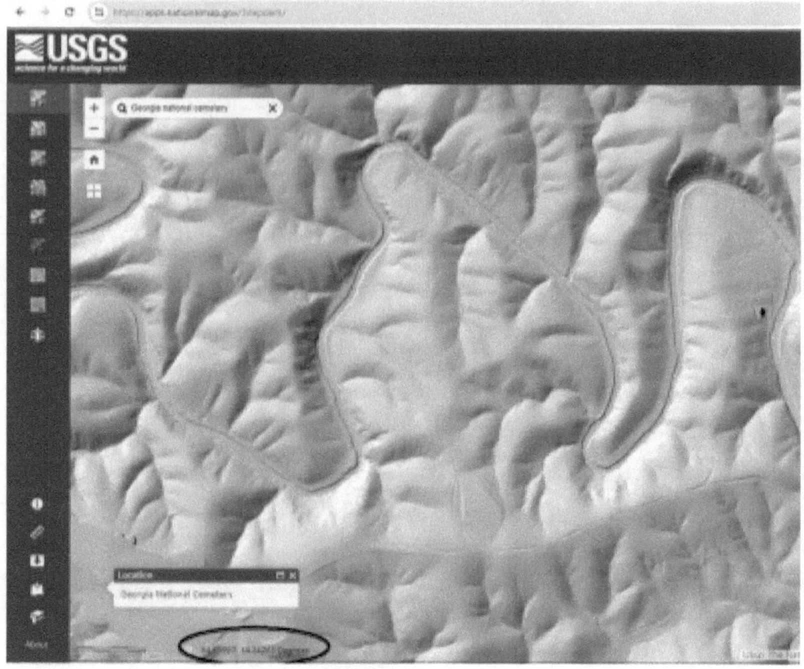

Display of area with hillshade layer toggled.

Place your cursor over the object in question and retrieve the latitude and longitude coordinates from the lower left of the screen.

As you discern from the contrast from the image on the left, parts of forest completely cover the visibility of the furnace. The path and road are different because the trees are gone. However, the LiDAR allows you to see through the vegetation perfectly. It should be noted that at this level of resolution, manmade objects must be large to jump out at you. The furnace is shaped like a trapezoid, 28 feet high and 28 feet wide from side to side.

My daughter Aviana at the collapsed eastern side

Go to Google and enter the Latitude and Longitude. Click on the Maps tab and look for directions with a car. Drive out to the closest location that allows you the safest and shortest distance to the site. In this case, the cemetery itself. When you arrive and park as close as you can, change the direction medium from car to hiking.

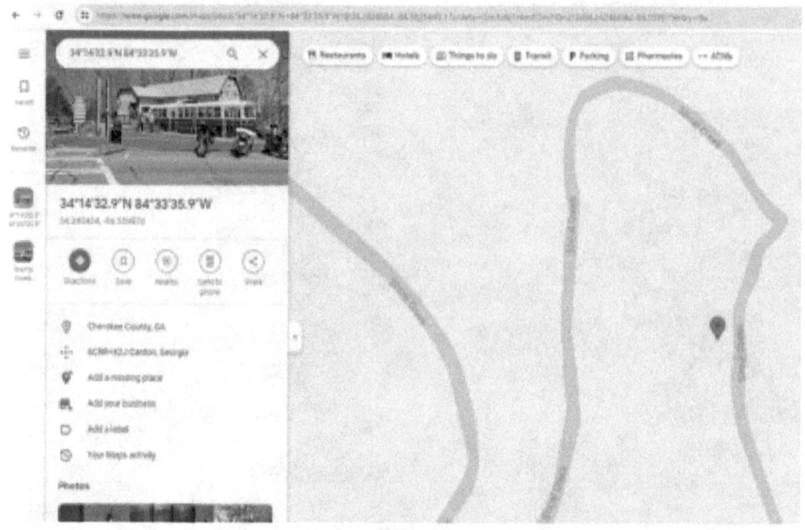

Google Maps view of latitude and longitude

Rural Exploration – Part 4:

(The 50,000-foot view)

In the three previous sections, I elaborated on different steps and tools you could use to find old homesteads: maps, photographs, technology, and trees, plants, and other natural features.

There's one other important component for exploration: having the correct perspective.

In literary analysis, you must use different tools and clues to understand the author's intention: political, cultural, social and economic environment, biases, etc. This field of study is called hermeneutics, named after the Greek messenger god Hermes.

Take a similarly multifaceted approach when exploring a site. Do not make the mistake of viewing a property from your modern perspective.

Look for things that all humans need to live - water, food, shelter, and warmth. In the days before refrigeration, we had fresh-water springs (and ice if we lived far enough north) and family cemetery plots. Before automobiles and refrigeration, family plots near the house were far more common. In the days before grocery stores, we had gardens, cattle, and fish. In the days before indoor plumbing, we had outhouses. In the days before central heating, we had fireplaces. Searching for signs of a good homestead means looking for a giant shade tree to shelter and protect cattle (food), a fresh spring (water and refrigeration), shelter (rocks, logs, wood, mud), and a chimney (warmth, food preparation).

Depending on the age of the homestead, you may find advancements in technology: a well instead of a spring; the remnants of a wood-burning stove instead of/or in addition to a chimney; electric and phone lines instead of candles, lamps or only mail; air conditioning and refrigeration instead of a spring and ice box; indoor plumbing instead of well, spring and an outhouse.

Finding a homestead using nature's signs and then confirming the location later with maps: A Visual Guide.

The following is an example of a homestead I found:

Look for a giant oak, beech, or other hardwood with a high crown and massive trunk circumference. Look for evidence of a former driveway and whether, as on rare occasions, there might be a mailbox that had not been removed.

A giant shade tree is visible from the road. Note the perennials in front.

If in the Springtime, look for flowers close to the shade tree. If you see perennials, you can be assured you're on the right track. Keep searching near the perennials and you may discover more. Near these flowers I discovered a wooden fence with hog wire built in, probably to contain animals or to keep animals out of a garden.

A wooden fence with hogwire mesh was located less than ten feet
from the perennials

A cinder block foundation with more perennials.

Finally, I found my favorite part of my homestead exploration, the chimney—in this case a double-sided chimney with a brick insert. It was designed to heat more than one room and may have doubled as a heat source for a bedroom and living room.

Angela studies the various materials used in the construction of a chimney

The different materials in the chimney indicate it was added onto over many years as standard building materials changed. The lower section of the outside was older than the top section. This chimney wasn't faced with material. It was modified at least twice over the decades it stood.

An old chimney with evidence of structural modifications over time. Not the differences at the base, insert, and top.

A set of wooden steps that once accessed an entrance

It also has a set of steps that at one time allowed access to an entrance about a foot off the ground.

In conclusion, given the condition and materials used in the construction of the house, chimney, fences, and equipment, I evaluated the homestead as being from the early 20th century, likely between 1900 and 1920. Although, there is a chance more than one structure was built here, given the differences in materials used in the chimney and the age of the trees.

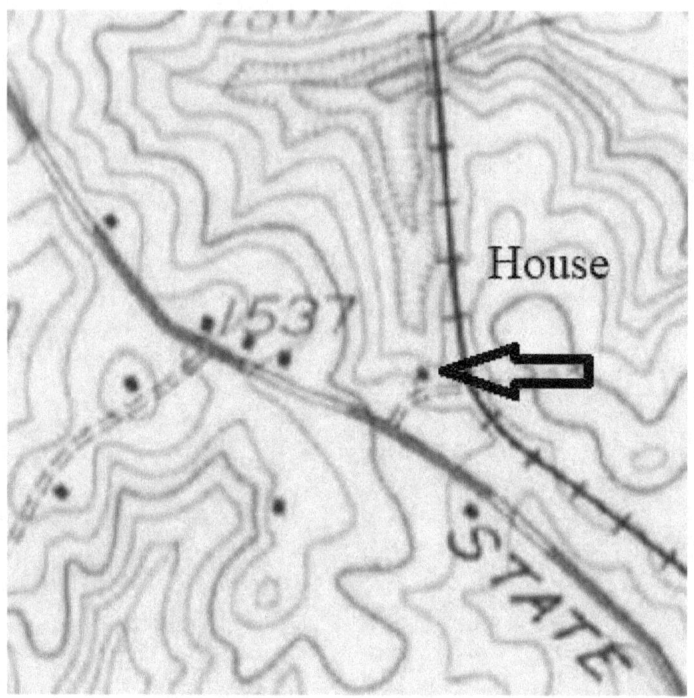

The 1926 Tate Quadrangle Topographic map shows the house.

Neither the previous county map from 1903 from JW Henley nor any of the previous topographic maps from the 1800s show the house. The ruins are located on Land Lot 269, District 12 of Pickens County.

The land records show that the last seller of the property was Mrs. Kimberly Jarvis. Kimberly was the daughter of Mary Jones Bryant. Mrs. Bryant's maiden name was Jones. Her family's brick house sits to this day on a hill across Talking Rock Road from the discovered property. Mary Jones was married to James P. "Pete" Bryant. He tragically died on November 23, 1973, at the age of 32 from exposure to gases in the well of the property.

In wells, as with other enclosed spaces, the deeper and narrower they are, the less oxygen they'll have. If someone spends too much time in one, they'll convert too much oxygen to carbon dioxide. At that point, they can die from poisoning.

This type of poisoning is referred to as "confined space hypoxic syndrome."

The Distance Between

Our loved ones did the best they could (or so we tell ourselves).

And yet invariably the truth remains alone.

We made excuses for those we loved,

while pretending their faults were not their own.

But choice remained, where fate could not,

lest we dare explore...

them not loving us as much as they could.

(but only as much as they tried)

And the distance mattered more.

We loved them each for all they gave,

but our memories remained intact,

and as trying as it was to realize,

we could not ignore the facts.

What was the same for you, was the same for all.

From the Garden of Eden to the Fall,

from the mother to child, husband and wife,

lovers and the loved, and each separate life.

They loved you not as much as they could

but only as much as they tried.

But as far as our delusions were concerned,

to ourselves we hadn't lied.

Afterword

As I delved deeper into history, I discovered two realities:

1) The world with all its moving parts is far more interconnected than seems possible at first glance. Beneath the surface of what ostensibly seem to be disparate events are threads of social, economic, and geographic forces that bind us to each other. They are inseparable.

2) Truth is not only stranger than fiction, it is far more savage. Social strata, socioeconomic disparity, and the chaos of the genetic lottery play a determinative role in how you are treated in life and death. These rules follow you from the cradle to the grave. Some of us are deliberately ignored, lost, or forgotten by the machinery of systemic power dynamics. This lesson is the hardest to discern, and the toughest to ignore once you see it. Like an optical illusion that reveals a hidden character, once you see it, you cannot unsee it.

By sharing my love of history, I pray the events I've expounded upon will remove the veil from my readers' eyes, if only for a moment. And if doing so encourages them to pursue their own learning adventures and quests for truth, all the better.

Have fun and be well.

Christopher Feldt

Jasper, Georgia,

2024

About the Author

Chris Feldt is a father, veteran, artist, writer, researcher, poet, composer, and history buff. He moved with his daughter Aviana to North Georgia in 2018.

Read more at https://www.northgeorgiahistory.com.